I0580785

Unsettled

ISBN 978-1-7354999-6-3
Library of Congress Control Number: 2024942825
Published by Benicia Literary Arts
Benicia, California
www.benicialiteraryarts.org

Benicia Literary Arts, founded in 2012, encourages reading and writing in the community by producing events, creating a community of writers and readers, encouraging their development, and publishing works of high quality in all genres.

Editors: Mary Susan Gast and Mary Eichbauer
Book design: Jan Malin
Cover image: Adobe Stock Photos

Special thanks to Sherry Sheehan and Roger Straw for additional help.

Printed in the United States of America

Dedication

To all the stalwart, dogged poets who, from 2020-2023, gathered electronically for First Tuesday sessions, for topical poetry readings, for Love Poetry celebrations, for ekphrastic events, who wrote for "Going The Distance" and the Joel Fallon Poetry Scholarship, who came up with ZipOdes, who would not be silenced by COVID's grim restrictions, who raised their voices—some found their voices— in face-offs with viral pandemic, racial injustice, economic hardship, climate crisis, and threats to democracy, who testified to the unifying power of art and story, the joys and frustrations of hard-won daily life, the depths of grief, and the delicate beauty within and around us. This volume is for you, with a poem of thanks and admiration.

Two-and-a-half Years of Virtual Real Poetry

Frail
Fragile
Dependent on whimsical Zoom,
Imperfectly connected.

Strong
Deep
Secured through
Voices
Faces
Hearts.

Community
Kinship
Lives lived
Prevailed over mindless conspiracies,
Freed us from isolation,
Overthrew every effort to keep us apart.

Mary Susan Gast

Introduction

What does it mean to feel unsettled? To have no home, no resting place? To feel like a bird in a storm, hopping from branch to branch, never returning to the nest?

The world has changed since 2020. Old fears have resurfaced with new urgency, and fresh fears have arisen. What recourse do we have when faced with chaotic times?

Art can create beauty and connection out of difficult experiences. Poetry expresses emotion in the moment and externalizes that emotion in ways that can be shared with others, that create meaning from the chaos of fear and apprehension. When we share our fears, we face them together and our isolation eases.

The world has changed since 2020, but we have changed, too. After our forced isolation, we found ways of bringing our community back together, whether through the imperfect medium of cyberspace, or through in-person gatherings— tentative at first, soon with more assurance, more permanence. Somehow, moving by instinct, we always come together to restore community, to remind each other with compassion and empathy of the bonds that link us.

Mary Susan Gast, the eighth poet laureate of Benicia, took office in 2020, at the start of what would prove to be an exceptionally challenging time. Forced to reimagine the Poet Laureate Program without in-person gatherings, including the longstanding First Tuesday poetry meetings at the library, she used Zoom to maintain connection, and solidarity, in the local poetry community. That the poets' group has stayed together, and even added to their number, is a testament to Mary Susan's leadership and persistence.

This book, compiled by Mary Susan of poems written by the First Tuesday Poets, presents an expression of the difficult times we have passed through and their antidote. The community of poets who have written these words offer them to you as a record of their refusal to submit to despair or to lose hope through a long, difficult moment.

We are "unsettled," but not defeated. Shaken, but standing firm.

Mary Eichbauer
Editor-in-Chief, Benicia Literary Arts

Table of Contents

AzzaMariem Abdou

AzzaMariem Abdou is a Benicia High School alum, attending Chico State University as a freshman pre-nursing major. Azza hopes to complete her dreams by becoming a pediatric nurse. She has been writing poetry and other texts since she could pick up a pencil, and she plans on continuing with her love of poetry by writing and performing for years to come. She is Benicia High School's 2023 recipient of the Joel Fallon Poetry Scholarship.

Apart from school and writing poetry, Azza volunteers as a youth cheerleading coach and devotes lots of her time to creating award-winning routines for teams ages 8–14. She began volunteering as a coach in 2019 with Benicia's Youth Football & Cheer organization and continued doing so through graduation. She currently coaches with Chico's Junior Panther organization.

Exactly

How do I become something that Love wants to come home to?
       —Stay exactly as you are.
Now this does not mean *stop evolving*
This means stay living as you are.
Stay as alive as the ocean against its shore,
Repeatedly rejected, but ever so more intrigued.
This does not mean *go back to dead ends*
Keep your sense of wonder, wonder what will happen if you try again.
Remember this does not mean *convince,* this does not mean *force,*
Wonder softly
Be *alive* in every breath
Dance to the rhythm of the silence between sentences,
This does not require a personal redesign,
This does not require any more time,
This does not require—
How do I become something that Love wants to come home to?
       —You are.

Little Girl/Big Girl

When I grow up, I want really long hair.
& I want to be a singer,
I hope I get to meet Michael Jackson!
When I grow up, I want to be like her,
I can't wait until I can wear makeup!
I can't wait until I can wear high heels.
When I grow up, I swear I'm still going to play dolls,
Mom, I'm not little anymore!

AzzaMariem Abdou

When I grow up, I hope I'm as pretty as her.
I can't wait until I'm older,
I'm so excited for high school.
When I grow up, I want to be an author.
When I grow up, I want to be a pilot.
I can't wait until I can drive,
Mom, I hate that, I'm not a little girl anymore!

When I grow up, I hope I'm skinnier
& I can't wait until I have my own car,
I'm so excited for senior pictures.
I can't wait to graduate,
When I grow up, I want to be successful,
When I grow up, I want to help kids.
Mom, stop! I'm not a little girl anymore!

I drive. I graduated,
But when I grow up, I want to be a pediatric nurse.
I wear high heels, I don't play dolls,
But when I grow up, when I finish college,
I want to be a mom.
I can't wait to have my own house,
When I grow up, I'm still going to be a kid.
When I grow up, I hope I'm fearless.

AzzaMariem Abdou

Pieces of Pieces

Shaped
Molded
This is what you'd say about this girl at first glance
But look closer,
I am sculpted.
Carved.
Mastered to the people I walk by,
Built by boys who scratch my heart.
I am woodwork,
Art.
Built from the suffrage of you
Painted from escaping your wounds,
Put together by saltwater air and her cigarette ash,
I am pieces of pieces
From here and from Egypt
I am pieces of pieces
Of treasure and trash
I am pieces of pieces
Of smiles and pain,
Of laughter untamed,
I am pieces of pieces
Of the pieces of you.

AzzaMariem Abdou

Melody Anderson-Brumidis

Melody loves reading stories to her granddaughter Sofia, 3. Her grandson's smile—Lil Leo, six months old—makes her day. She also enjoys walking her five chihuahua mixes and playing with her calico cat Meow Meow. Gardening is one of her passions.

An avid reader, Melody looks forward to a book of poems with her name on it. After retirement, she was embraced by the Solano poets. She's an active member of Poetry by the Bay, Benicia's First Tuesday Poetry, and the Poetry Book Club, which studies famous poets. She served on the committee to select Vallejo's Poet Laureate in 2023.

Loretta, Melody's wife of 36 years, is her rock. Long-term residents of Vallejo, they adopted and raised five children. Their now grown children—Khalea, 27; Khaleo, 26; Maxx, 23; Alisha, 19; and Kody,18—provide material for Melody's poems. She hopes you enjoy her poems in this book.

Like a Queen

One lazy summer Sunday
Treat me like a queen
What does that mean?
Let me sleep in
Until the sunlight peeks
Through the window
And grazes my shut eyes

Let the smell of fresh coffee
Tickle my nose
Be as excited to see me
As my 5 chihuahua mixes are
Bark, all together now
Run in circles
Wag your tail

Serve me breakfast in bed
Bright big red strawberries
Cut in a bowl
Raisin toast
Topped with a pat of butter
And freshly squeezed orange juice

Watch as I slowly open my eyes
And marvel at your kindness
Smile, silently smile at me
Place the Sunday *Chronicle*
On the bed next to me
Allow me to take in
This scene
Like the queen
I am

Melody Anderson-Brumidis

Don't Cry for Me

My dog Marley is out
of this world
and yet I see her everyday
when I go out in the backyard.
Sun shining down on me, I see
Marley's rubber bones and
raise my head to the sky and cry, "Hi Marley."

Marley is the happiest dog
  in dog heaven.
There she can do no wrong.
Here she played catch with me with
  her four rubber bones every day
up to 100 catches at a time.

Now her rubber bones lie lonely
  because not one of my five
other dogs will play catch with me.
If only Marley had learned
  to be kind and gentle
  with the other dogs,
she'd be here now.

"Don't cry for me," Marley says
  in a language we both understand.
"In dog heaven, I run as fast
as I can, catch 1,000 rubber bones,
  and eat manna—seven types of meat."

"Smile, smile when you think of me!"

Melody Anderson-Brumidis

The Poet's Tear

I am a poet, and
I have my own emotions.
No one can take them away from me.
When I show my emotions, I hear
"You're the one tripping on it."

And, I too can become a robot.
Artificial Intelligence (AI) runs the world.
ChatGPI does my children's homework
from kindergarten on.
No need to cheat anymore.
AI will do it for you.

The poets are still there amongst us.
Like dandelions they pop up bright yellow flowers,
white puffballs when you least expect them.
The deep feelers, the empaths will always be here
writing around deer-head chihuahuas who sit on their laps.

The poems are dripping with emotions, sensations.
The senses multiply 5 x 5, 25 x 10, 250.
The robots look, but do not see.
The poet gently takes the stiff silver
hand of the robot, and allows it to feel the poet's tear, one of many.

Melody Anderson-Brumidis

Claire J. Baker

Claire J. Baker, long active in the Bay Area poetry scene in varied arenas of service, is most proud of promoting Poetry Landmarks to honor California's first Poet Laureate, Ina Donna Coolbrith, who as a librarian mentored Jack London and other aspiring writers. The venerable Coolbrith Circle still thrives. Also, Claire worked with the California State Library in Sacramento, securing space for member books, preserved in perpetuity in the Coolbrith Circle Special Collection.

Devoted to poetry since the 1950s, Claire, naming "poetry" as having saved her life, has logged over five thousand poems printed, with more than 400 contest placements. Presently an elder-elder, Claire serves on the Board of The Circle. And she still avidly sends out her work.

A Shimmering

High in the sky a shimmering
in wakes of a million fervent wishes,
as people pray both night and day,
hoping every word is heard.

In wakes of a million fervent wishes
we speak as if there were an angel
who listens, hears our every word
in sun-bright lighting of a cloud.

You speak as if there were a saint,
dear one. And you believe there is
in sun-bright lighting of a cloud,
mystical and other worldly.

Dear one, you believe there is
a portal where one kneels and waits,
feels mystical and otherworldly,
and are handed heaven's map—

a portal where you come and wait.
When your anticipation flares
you are holding heaven's map,
watching stars encircle darkness.

Again, anticipation flares
past life on earth, and now you kneel
as stars enliven all the darkness....
High in the sky a shimmering.

Grand Prize, Dancing Poetry Festival, July 2023

Claire J. Baker

Seekers

Seekers of the exotic, riders
and writers of water & wind,
shapers of jewels and jazz,
builders of bridges and ball fields,
explorers of the psyche,
embryos this moment conceived—

whatever we believe tomorrow,
in a hundred years, or
on the last turn of the earth
under moonlight's incantations—
visionaries, may we lean
toward the language of roses.

Claire J. Baker

Border Crossing
From Central America

All the lost children,
who trudged long and far,
families fleeing
violence, gangs, war,
all beg asylum,

nos rescataras. . .
All the lost children
arriving worn-out
at guarded borders,
yanked from hurt parents—

por que y donde,
like quarantined sheep!
All the lost children
shipped off or caged in
tents, the heat intense—

innocent victims:
twenty-three hundred
suffering traumas.
All the lost children
left to cope alone.

History depicts
these migrant martyrs,
political pawns…
Hordes wept, still weep for
all the lost children.

                                    Claire J. Baker

Ilean Baltodano

Ilean Baltodano is a child of the Universe, God
Nobody else has her fingerprints
She is proud of the color of her skin: "Brown Sugar"
She was born in Nicaragua
Worked for Exxon
Started a family
Attended Law School
Universidad Centroamericana, Nicaragua
Bachelor and Master Degrees, University of San Francisco CA

Ilean seeks a purpose for her life. She travels domestically and around the world. Traveling gives her a vast education into new cultures, religion, history, food, and especially people. It reminds her that we are all human beings. As an immigrant, she has experienced how hard it is to migrate while looking for freedom and safety. Even though she is in the autumn of her life, she has the energy to speak up on behalf of Nicaragua via her channel on YouTube. She has a pragmatic way of looking at life.

I.—Introvert
L.—Latina
E.—Endures
A.—American
N.—Nicaraguan

Immigrant Plow the Land

Immigrant come!
Come with your strong hands
With your unreachable dreams
With your fears and tireless struggles
With your culture

Come to nurture the drought of this land
Come to caress the earth
Open the grooves like half-open lips
Fill the creases with the seed of your yearnings
Soak the furrows with tears and blood

Sing to Mother Earth with your guitar
With your desires this land will flourish
Even if later, they snatch the harvest from you
Even if later,
They seize you for being undocumented

Mother Earth…
The mother of all creatures
Mother Earth…
Gives life to those who caress her skin
For Mother Earth…WE ARE ALL EQUAL

                                    Ilean Baltodano

The Holocaust Happened

This is a harsh reality
An incomprehensible chapter in history
Let's fight antisemitism,
hostility, prejudice, and bigotry
Listen, new generation
children, grandchildren and
great grandchildren:
The Holocaust happened
The Gas Chamber happened
The survivor's sentiment
is sad and tragic
New generations, be aware
There is good and evil in the world
Let's fight for the helpless
Let's teach the unhuman: humanity
Let's destroy the powerful evil
Let's fight for honesty and reverence
There is real love as well
Let's not forget
The Holocaust happened!

Ilean Baltodano

Black History is the American History

Black History is the story of the USA society
Of migration, slavery, and lynching
Of injustice and abomination
The Black History in USA
Is a chapter that cannot be deleted nor edited
It is written in the indelible ink of tears and blood

Black History is full of heroes
Ida B. Wells
Harriet Tubman
Martin Luther King, Jr.
Rosa Parks
Maya Angelou

These and many more belong
in our children's school curriculum
Let's continue intoning
"I have a dream"
To make Martin Luther King's
dream come true!

Ilean Baltodano

Peter Bray

Peter Bray is a graduate of UC Berkeley and a Benicia resident since 1983. He's written and published three chapbooks and has 16 original songs on Youtube.com. He's written a column, "The A Cappella Handyman—The Poetry Guy," for the *Benicia Herald* since 2008 and won the Benicia Love Poetry Contest that same year. He's a member of Benicia's First Tuesday Poets and Benicia Literary Arts. His creative newsletter, *Taproot & Aniseweed—The Naked Oyster* has been in nearly continuous publication since 1987.

Words 'n Birds

Words 'n birds take me aloft,
there so high where clouds are soft.
A daily flight beyond this stuff,
words 'n birds can't get enough.
Playing tag within my mind,
words 'n birds, we'll soon unwind.
Up, beyond and fly away,
words 'n birds, please come today.

Peter Bray

Two Right Shoes

Two right shoes, two right shoes,
I never get the blues with two right shoes.
I never shake hands with my left hand,
my daddy is a funny man.
Two left shoes, two left shoes,
I never have to choose with two left shoes.
I never have to pay my union dues,
whenever I wear my two left shoes.
Take a family member off to the zoo.
You can see giraffes and the elephants too.
You can always wonder what I'm gonna do,
whenever I wear my two right shoes.

Peter Bray

The Compost News Blues

Rockets and vessels and algae stew,
these are the things that I once drew.
Didn't make LIFE nor the cover of TIME,
but the Compost News had a cover of mine.
10,000 copies went through the mail,
a shower of glory or was it hail?
No Golden Record upon my wall,
but the Compost News hangs there for all.
No, I didn't make LIFE nor the cover of TIME,
but the Compost News thinks I'm divine!

Peter Bray

Suzanne Bruce

Suzanne Bruce holds a B.S. in Education from the University of Tulsa and did graduate work in Behavior Disorders at Wichita State University. Suzanne has been the MC for the Solano County Library Foundation's Authors Luncheon for 6 years. In 2022, she conducted an on-stage conversation with author Amy Tan. Her poems have won several prizes and she has been published in numerous journals, such as *Copperfield Review, Phati'tude, Suisun Valley Review* and *Interlitq*. Her books, *Voices Beyond the Canvas* (2007) and *Her Visions Her Voices* (2015), are ekphrastic duets with artist Janet Manalo (www.ekphrasticexpressions.com). She is the current Poet Laureate for the city of Fairfield, California.

Bodega Bay Get-Away

we rush to get there

zip past mustard-yellow carpets
of Napa Valley floors
zing through Petaluma
eagerly greet roads past town
where sunshine winks through
deep-green needles
and piney fragrances flourish
zigzag the winding coastal road
that leads us to the place

                        where time goes on hold

amber and emerald succulents
dress the rugged russet cliff
our vacation house proudly
protects us from demanding
                        spring winds

while a restless ocean plays tag
with each incoming and outgoing
wave   a sneaky fog
                        erases the horizon

like we sometimes wish
we could do.

                                    Suzanne Bruce

Uncertainty

One step   then another
unbridled trail lined
with feathering ferns
I stop
        look up
towering limbs
  shadow all beneath
earthy fragrance pervades
how these giants
      once seedlings
stay alive   so old
still luscious   a mystery
I press my hand
against fibrous bark
revel in the majesty   the divine
dapple-gray clouds
look
    down
tingly mist touches my face
then processions of golden sunrays
           jet
make me squint   think
belief is stronger than expectation
efforts denser than regret
uncertainty has an origin
every origin creates a new step

Suzanne Bruce

Afterwards

Cleaning out should be easy
after all   I had been wanting to do it for years
what has gone before is streaming into the invisible
timeless and good however bitter it may seem
our mother-daughter relationship
like a pendulum   only uneven swinging

now that you have passed   a slow caress of years begins
a journey flowing into a path worn by other waters

I rummage through your paid bills statements
records of doctor's appointments
tax papers   even your covid test results—

Sorting these no longer needed files
papers now piled high on the floor
but were you more than documents
      I did keep you safe and organized

I pretend to not notice the shadows
memories like a restless child turning   and   turning
the lump in my stomach   the pain I did not expect to feel

voices echo in the misty valleys of my heart
as day progresses into night
                  bright specks light the darkness
as my pulse flows with new unknown
like a star that sees beyond her own light
                              for the first time

                                    Suzanne Bruce

Jim Cotter

Jim Cotter is a poet and YA novelist who enjoys outdated lyricism and poetry as argued history. He writes a lot about the internet, 24-hour news cycle, and narwhals. He has previously been published in *Sparkle* and *Blink* and is the author of *Push Notifications* and *Kid Ninja and the Idunn Conspiracy*. He lives in Benicia with his spouse and two children.

Narsmhals

The miniature narwhal, or narsmhal,
also known as Dalton's Narwhal,
was first discovered in Charing Cross
by Gerald Dalton, a tax collector
and natural science hobbyist.
In all ways they resemble their larger analogues
except that their horn,
is composed of a fine crystalline material.
Like their counterpart,
the horn is used to sense
changes in the atmosphere,
locate food, and secure mates.
The narsmhal was discovered somewhat by chance
when an eccentric and indigent friend of Dalton
repeatedly went ill after drinking from a decorative fountain.
When a kidney biopsy was taken,
cavorting narsmhals
could be seen at play
in the renal hilum.
They are quite prolific and exist in most
bodies of freshwater, though in concentrations
lower than that found in Charing Cross,
and generally in concentrations
insufficient to cause
the illness that led to their discovery.
Their song is said to be
lamentably sad,
and there is a legend
amongst those biologists
who study narsmhals
that it can drive one mad,
though it is happily below the threshold
of unassisted human hearing.

                    Jim Cotter

kiss me

kiss me in my living room

and harrow me on the porch
show me to your dining room,
and we'll complicate your best china pattern.
open up your dusty cupboards,
let's crawl where the knives lie down,
show me to your linens drawer,
in a sea of bleached stains,
we'll float untouched.
in the shower,
we'll press against the glass door like steam.
let's fill the house with us,
and fill ourselves with the house.
let my memories be rooms,
that i have to look for you in.

Jim Cotter

Rory Livesay Coyne

Rory Coyne is an 18-year-old who went to Benicia schools her whole life. Rory graduated from high school early. She has been writing poems since the second grade. She uses poetry to help with her mental health. She always keeps a journal and sparks ideas for her poetry from daily life. Rory aspires to have her work published one day. She plans to continue writing poetry for all of her life.

Lover

The waves breaking on the shore like to play a game of back and forth
The ocean on the west lets the sun stay the night
The ocean on the east says their relationship with the sun is better in
    the morning
The ocean that rests in the middle of the compass only sees the sun
    above
In all the ways the ocean knows the sun it sticks and repeats
It's a cadence, a slow beat that marches across the sky
On the cloudy days
The days where it seems the sun doesn't want to come out to play
Rise—Set
Wake—Sleep
Thump Thump, I can feel it
Each second shakes the earth
We have grown used to the idea of existence
There is a star in my sky
That looks over me like a father
Warms me like a mother
Breathing and being is mindless
Do you ever ask the sun
Where did you come from?

                                        Rory Livesay Coyne

Womanhood part 1

I open my mouth underwater
I am pale
Soon I turn blue
I'd like to say it's because I'm one with the ocean
My body could never be anything as angry as the sea
I may only be beautiful
Kind
My tongue may always bleed
My heart must always be resilient
Quietly

Rory Livesay Coyne

Womanhood part 2

I'm starting to feel my destiny as a woman is to create another. My life's work will pass as I nurse a child. It's the most fulfilling thing, they say. It will change your life, they say. It will. My life, my love, my legacy goes into a long white dress. A child-mined diamond ring for me to wear as a sign of completion. I want to be more. I want my words to fill souls. I want to be read, sung, and spoken. My mind is my art and all they see is my fertility. The love I'm supposed to give, the selflessness I'm meant to share. I am a woman with weight, a woman of my own. I'm more than my forging motherhood. My mother is more than my birth. Lisa, Lisa with a last name passed down by fathers who watched their children be raised. Lisa, the words roll out. She is not only my mother. She is an educator, a college graduate, a survivor, my peace of mind. She is my best friend. She passed down more than her life. I wish she knows she's more than the life she's given me. I want to be more than the life I give. My title is not only to be a mother, however the name my mother gave me.

Mary Eichbauer

Born in New York City, Mary Eichbauer makes her home in Benicia, California. She holds a B.S. from Caltech and an M.A. and Ph.D. from UCLA in Comparative Literature. Her first book of poetry, *After the Opera*, was published by Random Lane Press in 2020. Other publications include articles, book reviews, and a book of literary criticism entitled *Poetry's Self-Portrait: The Visual Arts as Mirror and Muse in René Char and John Ashbery* (1992). With Johanna Ely, Laurie Hailey, and Deborah Bachels Schmidt, she co-authored the poetry anthology *Love's Meditation*. She is currently working on a memoir and a second poetry collection. Her poems have been recognized with awards from the Poets' Dinner and the Ina Coolbrith Circle Contest. She currently serves as Editor-in-Chief of Benicia Literary Arts.

Public Service Announcement

From now on in the city center
tourists will enjoy only pure experiences—
sharp as a blade,
bracing as the slap of an ocean wave.

When you nestle an espresso cup
in the palm of your hand,
the heat of it will settle there
at the base of your thumb,
right where you need it most.

Mary Eichbauer

Summer Thunder in Paris

Another leisurely afternoon at a café
waiting for the thunder to decide
whether to stop growling
and open the skies
or to keep things uncertain a little longer.

Back home, the hours
between lunch and dinner
go by in a flash, full of work
and nothing in particular.
The pitiless California light
burns the time away,
as the cat on the rug
moves from sun to shade
and back again,
her golden eyes half-closed,
glowing little suns.

But here, in this ancient city—
this vessel, always
on the edge of shipwreck—
people sit outside,
happy to see the sun,
the long cold winter
not quite forgotten,
not quite despised,
the price to pay for this gift,
this warm afternoon
under an unsettled sky,
drinking a lemonade.

Mary Eichbauer

Persistence

On the path a nasty boy
throws rocks at birds.
He fashions a little spear
and sharpens it, but he doesn't know
about heft and balance,
so the wind blows his weapon away
time after time.

Up in their tree, nuzzling and cooing,
the wood pigeons don't know
that they could lose each other
any time.

Self-conscious, embittered,
the boy throws rocks,
half-sneering at himself
because he knows it's wrong,
but he needs to do it anyway,
to try over and over
until he has blood on his hands.

Mary Eichbauer

Johanna Ely

Johanna Ely is the author of four poetry books, *Transformation, Tides of the Heart—Poems for Benicia, Postcards From a Dream* (Blue Light Press 2020), and *What Still Matters* (Last Laugh Productions 2023). She is an award-winning poet who has been published in literary journals and anthologies, including *California Quarterly* and *The Poeming Pigeon*. She has been nominated for a Pushcart Prize, and was the 2022 winner of the Benicia Love Poetry Contest. Johanna served as the sixth poet laureate of Benicia, California, and is a board member of the Ina Coolbrith Circle of Poets, one of the oldest poetry groups in California.

Fragments

I wake to morning,
my bed filled with fragments
of other people's dreams.

Last night, a fragment of moon
kept me up late,
asking too many questions.

I wake to morning,
lost in the wreckage
of last night's insomnia—
fragments of memory bobbing
just out of reach.

Outside my window,
strangers talk and plan their day—
fragments of conversation
pierce my subconscious.

I wake to morning,
wondering who I am.

Johanna Ely

A Leaf is a Poem

The song you heard singing in the leaf
when you were a child
is singing still.
                    —Mary Oliver

A leaf is a poem
without words.
It is the universe
in constant motion—
shift of light, change of color,
cycle of birth and death.

A poem quivers
on a branch,
falls silently to the ground.
It cries without tears—
I weep and write it down.

Johanna Ely

The Trees at the State Park are Dying

I don't know their names,
only that they stand in the meadow
beautiful and dead.
Wild poppies grow around them.

They died last winter,
some say from too much rain,
though they look drought-stricken—
their ash gray bones brittle and cracked,
skeletal branches twisting towards sky.

Does a heart still flicker
deep inside each trunk?
Does amber blood still flow,
or has the sap turned hard?
Gone, the soft breathy song
of leaves rustling in the wind.

A brazen fungus stains some trees
bright orange, covers tender skin
with blighted beauty.

Proof that life goes on—
is that what's understood?—

as crows caw loudly
perched on barren branches,
and beetles bore into
the rotting wood.

                                        Johanna Ely

Tyler Foy

Tyler Foy is a semi-recent adult & second-year college student majoring in both Studio Art & Foreign Language. He was a recipient of the 2022 Joel Fallon Poetry Scholarship, and since graduating high school has continued to write. He is now in the midst of finishing his last two semesters before he receives his Associate's degrees. After that, he'll be off to a four-year university. Between balancing school, jobs & staying somewhat sane, Ty writes—poetry, drafts of novellas that will never see the light of day, songs, D&D campaign ideas, thoughts & feelings.

Ty finds great comfort in writing & hopes to inspire others to give writing a try as a way to express themselves.

Idiosyncrasies

The shapes made by the sun as it casts shadows onto the grass
feel like nothing more than unchanging repetitions against the earth.

I find myself wondering why, to me, the world never felt infinite,
nor beautiful—
truthfully it never really felt like much at all.

I've been told that the color of the sky at sunset is one of the most
indescribable colors that the human eye can see.
I've stared at the sky, long and hard—
eyes squinting skyward, brimming with tears,
begging to see more than a simple red-orange.

Maybe there isn't a greater meaning to any of it,
But I still hold onto a glowing thread of hope—
hope that the beauty in the world will make itself known to my eyes
and fill my lungs with sweetness and vigor.

Tyler Foy

Paralysis

The sepia-toned images of childhood laughter and the innocent
bliss of my pre-teen years
fading away like the last rays of a dying sun.

I'm haunted by memories of people & places that are no longer here
like familiar ghosts of a life that isn't mine—
was never mine.

Their faces & voices echo in the recesses of my mind,
poisonous touches leaving a lingering sting in my spine.

Decay.

I've come to see time is unrelenting, refusing to stop or falter for
even a moment.

It marches forward with merciless indifference, dragging me
further & further away from the world I once knew.

It is all a distant dream.

Now on the threshold of the present, I stand,
stiller than I've been in a while.
I mourn for the days that have gone by, painfully.

I am aware that they can never return.

But the paralyzing fear of what's to come—
even minutes from now—
keeps me from moving forward.

Tyler Foy

September

It's September again
A handshake—
a 20-minute drive
from where we last met.
Smiling faces, tear-stained sleeves, laughing loudly

It's September
and I am different when I wake up in the morning
Sleep still surrounding my eyes
Breath steady and cold
And alive

The breaking point was the last we spoke.

The changing of my surroundings had begged me to stall.
I kept pressing forward, though, didn't I?

And now it's September again
And change still laps at my heels
But the waters don't bother me.

Tyler Foy

Deborah L. Fruchey

Deborah L. Fruchey is an author, editor and publisher of the micro-press Last Laugh Productions. She likes this end of her life much better than the other, and finds the sacred in many strange places.

Morning Fog

Mist gathers
trailing whispers and innuendoes
from billowing gauze sleeves.
It looks at me sideways
and drops its eyes
obscuring the edges
of everything.

Where
exactly
does the twig
become cloud?
Do the leaves on the end
disperse
like ink in water?

Are those liquid leaves
against my skin?

Deborah L. Fruchey

Mowing Day

All flesh is grass—
though there are more tender
and determined greens,
less prone to pucker up with weeds
and fraternize with fungoid things,
less rumpled and disinterested
less likely to huddle, miserable with mush,
in wintertime.

Renewed in Spring, sprightly
like grace notes on a flute

only to be cut short

Oh, but the yearning smell,
that ardent keening
offering faith to the air—
growth is all
and hope is
even in death—
for all flesh

Deborah L. Fruchey

Haunted by the Bad Times

In the beginning,
a relationship is a haunting.
He gives advice,
you hear criticism.

He asks politely
for you to stop
doing something:
you hear disgust.

He is late coming home:
you suspect abandonment.

Anxious about your good luck
you make getaway plans,
look for cheap apartments,
hoard old dishes and silverware.

For 20 years
I have suspected
that it will all end tomorrow.

Deborah L. Fruchey

Mary Susan Gast

Mary Susan Gast became Benicia's eighth Poet Laureate in 2020, as COVID overtook us. She launched the newspaper column "Going The Distance" as a means of giving voice to writers and, as it turned out, creating a community. From the tiny rural town of Baroda, Michigan, she has been drawn to diverse places and involvements as a theologian, community organizer, and human rights advocate.

Uncertain Inalienable Rights

Inalienable rights
Endowed by our Creator
Absolute
Sacrosanct
Unassailable
Life
Liberty
Pursuit of happiness.

Except, of course,
If you have likewise been endowed
With a functioning uterus.

In which case, your inalienable rights
Are up for alienation
Trumped and superseded
Any time
Any old time
Any young time
Egg and sperm meet
Within you.

If you should conceive,
Whatever the circumstances,
Nothing
Can keep you from becoming a birth mother—
Or die trying.

Conscripted,
For servitude to the dogma—all dapper,
In judicial robes and senatorial togas—
That a fertilized egg is a full human being,
And, you, pregnant person, are NOT.
These truths we hold to be self-evident?

                                     Mary Susan Gast

Maybe Today, 2020

I haven't cried yet.
About the coronavirus,
And the fears and limitations,
And death and loss,
And the glowering menace
On the horizon
That might be
The ash of lives and woodlands,
But could just as easily be
The existential omen
For humanity henceforth and forever shrouded
In pandemic.

I haven't cried yet.
But yesterday I saw a white butterfly
In mercurial dance mode
Above the sidewalk
My grandson and I once walked
To and from his grade school,
When his friends would join us
Babbling and running,
When the sky glinted blue with sunlight,
And dragonflies escorted us into magic realms.

I haven't cried yet.

But today may be the day.

Mary Susan Gast

Cave of Isolation
(After Psalm 130)

I wait for comfort.
My whole being waits,
Crying out,
From the depths
Of my discouragement
And sorrow,
Of my pain,
And regret.
My moaning
Echoes unsettlingly
In the surround-sound
Of the cave of isolation
That has sealed me in,
That has sealed my fate.

Free us from confinement,
Free us all as we free one another,
All who have sprung from
The Creator, that is, from
The Wellspring of Compassion,
The Heart of Well-Wishing Joy,
Whose ways we can follow and all be
Sprung.
Free.

Mary Susan Gast

Carol Gieg

Carol Gieg has written poetry and prose since she was a young girl.

She's been featured on Ozcat Radio, in the *Benicia Herald*, and in various anthologies: Benicia Literary Art's *Nooks and Crannies* and *Yearning to Breathe Free*...Gina Barreca's *Fast, Fallen Women*...Christopher Okemwa's *I Can't Breathe, a Poetic Anthology of Social Justice*, and others.

Carol graduated from Dartmouth College and earned master's degrees in social Welfare and Public Health at the University of California, Berkeley. She retired after 35 years practicing as a social worker and psychotherapist.

Carol's memoir is based on her survival of and recovery from a brain injury. *TBI-To Be Injured, Surviving and Thriving After a Brain Injury*, encourages victims to chart a course for living beyond medical expectations.

 Carol lives in Benicia, California with her husband. Her next book will provide management tools for caregiving loved ones with dementia.

False Friend

It is at once a loyal friend and fickle.
Always there when you're in need.
But leaving you worse off than before
it comes to your aid.

Promises made as your desire increases,
Duplicity its calling card.
Blinded by its clandestine subterfuge,
This is your only friend.
"Just one more!" it insists, wearing you down until finally,
You down a shot straight from the bottle,
Leaving you to flail in the mire of your loneliness.
It tempts you mercilessly,
"What the hell do you matter anyway?"
But you can't love anyone else
Until and unless, you first love yourself.

"Fight back!" I demand unwittingly.
 "How can you choose that over me?!"
Worse, I can't rescue you, I've tried.
 It only made matters worse.
But, my friend, I understand, finally,
Your resistance is a symptom of this medical problem.
You are not to blame.
Remember always that, even though I
despise what you are doing under its dominion,
I will always love who you are.

You are not alone.

                                    Carol Gieg

Friendship Is My Deity

Friendship is the source of hope, support, refuge and trust,
The sweet taste of righteousness opposing sour fruits of depravity.
Friendship is a rudder on the vessel of hope,
Steering steadfast and stable through a fog of despair.

Friendship is a refuge from division and loneliness,
A shelter against separation from those we hold dear.
Friendship is a buttress of faith restored,
Supporting crumbling walls flooded by doubt.

Friendship is its own inimitable work of art,
One nearly destroyed by those without conscience.
Fanatics naively crazed and misled,
By a force of narcissistic intent.

The very worst characteristics that humanity can boast,
Its soldiers armed with isolation, enmity and hatred,
Will never defeat Friendship's battalion of compassion and empathy,
Friendship is my deity, ever victorious on the battlefield of Life!

Carol Gieg

Constricting

Vibrant and vicious insults
Woven gossamer threads of disdain.
Warp and weft of duplicity,
Desperately she tries to shoulder the blame.

"Sorry," doesn't begin to unravel,
"Sorry for apologizing" does no more.
Hopeless, she tries to discover,
Isn't there anything she can apologize for?

The shroud of antipathy shrinks tighter and tighter,
Setting her up, the closures that won't release.
What burdens her most is not living with death,
Only friendships offered, then retracted.

She tugs gently and, oh, so slowly,
The stitching sound, but the outer layer peels.
Revealing welts from being burned once again,
Some sorrowful memories never heal.

I pray to my heavenly Father,
Through Him, the strictures finally release.
May I be happy, may I be safe,
Oh please, dear G-d, let my heart find peace.

Carol Gieg

Brandon L. Greene

Brandon L. Greene is a writer, lawyer, artist and advocate. Originally from Las Vegas, Brandon has used his creativity since he was a kid to interpret and process his world as well as to imagine new possibilities. Art has always been his way of being his most vulnerable self in a world in which men and Black men in particular are rarely given permission to do so.

He often performs under his stage name, Pro-lyphek (or Pro-Dash for short):

> Prosperity is the
> Result
> Of
> Learning
> Yourself and
> Pursuing a
> Higher
> Elevation of
> Knowledge

Algorithms and Awe

I have never been inspired or in awe of someone I dated
Saying this out loud begs so many questions about my choices,
I know
I've reflected on this a lot, about the sheer happenstance, location
proximity, acceptance,
standard and such that drive this truth
But I've reconciled it all as I reflect on you
It's so strange that despite our proximity and shared people in common
It took an app, an act of faith, an algorithm, a log in
Things I fundamentally didn't believe in
To find something, someone for whom I am all in
It's really amazing, if you just pause and think about it
I had mostly lost faith and was using the app as a way to pass time
Maybe find someone to experience some new place that I wanted
to go to but didn't want to do so alone
With the understanding that wherever the situationship docked
I would be alone
I was actually cool with this
Love, vulnerability, expectations seemed far too risky
But then I saw your profile and well those thoughts got glitchy
All at once I was confronted with some questions about my
confidence and ego
I was so taken aback by your beauty but convinced that your inbox
was fully stocked
But that Leo overconfidence whispered (go ahead, take a shot)
And so I did but not immediately and fully expecting rejection
But then you replied and began our first chat session
Despite what seemed like a vibe I fully expected the conversation
to slowly die down to a trickle
Instead you sent me your number with the invitation to further
explore our connection
I still remember the day, you called and I heard your voice,

Brandon L. Greene

I was smitten
But I couldn't let you know that, we hadn't even met yet
So we continued to text until one night I asked
Are you open for brunch, could we meet at last
To my surprise you said yes
So I scrambled to find a suitable place that I hoped would impress
Or at least not ruin the new love interest
I remember feeling corny, standing in a suit jacket with flowers
Then I saw you walking towards me and thinking I could watch her
for hours
Then leaving the meal wondering how you might feel
But being so excited to tell my cousin, I think I found her, she's real
I was too scared or too cool, for something to say
I hope that day was the first day of an infinite string of every days
So we continued to meet, to date, to explore and each time I felt
me wanting you more
But I was fearful because we had reached that place
Where the potential for hurt could no longer be erased
No amount of playing it cool would allow me to save face
If for some reason you determined, we had completed our race
But to my surprise and delight you have remained
Such a blessing, a light, an antidote to the pain
I never would have thought that random 0s and 1s
Or a profile picture with prompts could lead me to feel things that
none before had
Such pride, such awe
Such belief that the trials, the mistakes, the flaws
Were perfectly orchestrated, divinely timed
Randomly generated for this unique find
A beautiful soul
Breathtakingly made
For me to experience
What a privilege that is
The internet age gave me something as timeless as this

Brandon L. Greene

Reflections at 40ish

Recently, I have been reflecting on my 40 years
Thinking about all the ways I do and do not align with my peers
All the many ways I feel like a success or abject failure
The ways in which comparison
Has warped my sense of self to be narrowly tailored
In many ways I'm blessed, lucky, highly favored
The universe has shined upon me
But on a day to day basis
I feel small, insecure, uninspired, devoid of the fun me
The pandemic years have been long, hard, unimaginable in
respects
Thick with the fog of pain, disorientation, loss of self, regret
In other ways it's been rejuvenating, filled with new found wonder,
discovery, joy, self respect
At 40ish, I've done all the things of teenage dreams
Kids, house, dog, degrees
And things of adult angst
Divorce, burials, really, deeply seeing me
I've lost touch with friends as success has come
Wondered if lost time with my grandparents rendered it all in vain
I've felt shame for choices and the permanence they've wrought
Then pride for surviving and augmenting the plot
I've rediscovered me now and accepted who was
Kept promises to travel, to live, to love
This reflection at 40ish is really to say
I've learned to embrace the now, the gift of today
And to not fear tomorrow, come what may
I'm certain this may change, things may get tricky
And I'll reflect much differently when 40ish meets 50

Brandon L. Greene

Beth Grimm

Beth Grimm is a local Benician involved actively in literary and creative arts. She says she's not a poet, but when the mood strikes her and she's looking for a way to express emotions in the fewest words possible, she turns to poetry. She spends the rest of her time writing prose, mainly nonfiction, memoir and family stories, and little books that inspire creativity. Her most recently published written works appear in BenLit anthologies, a column in the *Benicia Herald* called "The Benicia Walker," Mary Susan Gast's "Going the Distance" column in the *Benicia Herald*, and her published book, *The Great Grandpa Chronicles*. She's also active in the Arts community and her art and books can be seen at The Little Art Shop and The Depot in Benicia.

Winter is Coming

We made it to October
The heat of summer is finally gone
But… Winter is Coming

There's an abundance of adversity
redundancy
morbidity
Enough to go around

Waaa… waaaa
Wammalammabamma…
What're you gonna do till the cows come home?

You can sing, you can dance
You can cry, you can try
You can do something new.

You can ask someone, anyone
What can I do for you?
To get your mind off yourself
off your troubles
on the right track.

You can act, you can write,
You can sing, you can dance
You can cry, you can try…
To not follow the pack.

Beth Grimm

Try a random act of kindness
or toy, with seeking joy.
Laugh at yourself.
Make a face, tell a joke
Make someone else laugh.

It doesn't make you wrong
To look for what's right
What's good
What little thing you can do.

It doesn't mean you're ignoring the world's problems
Or turning your back on those who are wronged
Ignoring the downtrodden
Being ungodly
Refusing to be real.

What's real anyway?
Crying?
Condemning?
Criticizing?
Complaining?
Lamenting?
Whining?

Beth Grimm

Or,
Refusing to hate
trying to understand
To go on
To pray
To love

To remember how to smile
To help shovel a path
through the mire, just a section
Turn the tide, help the pendulum
Start its arc back in the right direction.

You can sing, you can dance
Winter is coming.
There's plenty of bad news in the air.
Waaa… waaaa
Wammalammabamma…
What're you gonna do till the cows come home?

You have a choice.

                                    Beth Grimm

Evie Groch

Evie Groch, Ed.D., enjoys writing poetry, short stories, memoirs, opinion pieces and letters to the editor. She enjoys humor and honed hers in presentations and writing. She also enjoys recipes, cooking, word challenges, and puzzles. She currently hosts cohort sessions for new administrators at Cal State East Bay.

Evie serves as the current president of the Ina Coolbrith Circle of poets, established in 1919. Her work has appeared in *The New York Times,* the *San Francisco Chronicle*, the *Contra Costa Times,* and online venues. Many of her poems are found in published anthologies such as: *Soul Poet Society—Quintessence Anthology, My Robot & Me Anthology, My Father Taught Me Anthology,* and *Touching, Poems of Love Anthology*.

Evie engages in the themes of travel, language, immigration, and justice. She peppers her writing with words from a variety of world languages, several of which she speaks. She is the author of *What Do You Bring to the Table?* and the recently published poetry book, *Half the Hurricanes*.

Reversal of Misfortune

*"Confusion is a word we have invented for an order which is
not understood."*—Henry Miller

I precede myself in time and space
I'm not on standard dials
Run me backwards to catch my drift
Read me from right to left

I am the thunder before the lightning
The bite before the bark
The crashing tree before the axe
The scream before the pain

I am the flying golf ball before the "fore"
The bleeding before the cut
The burial before the slaughter
The echo before the sound

I am PTSD before the combat
The scar before the surgery
The indigestion before the meal
The effect before the cause

I am the prayer for forgiveness before the sin
The damage before the warning
The nightmare before the Holocaust
By the time you hear me, it's already too late.

                                                     Evie Groch

Where Learning Lies

Off the main road
in the pockets of slopes
between seams in fields
we tread with caution
on uneven paths
pounding gravel
with soles of sturdy sandals

We seek not the din
but the deserted decibel
not the force
but the fictive footnotes

We avoid crushing fauna
swerve around the lounging lizard
let lotuses lie on peaceful ponds

We inhale succulent scents
exhale warm breath
spot camouflaged chameleons
bask on sunlit stone slabs

Wildflowers welcome us
birdsongs greet us
We saunter back to the road home
enter into evening
with a renewed sense
of belonging, recognizing
a new tenor in our being,
knowing better who we are

Evie Groch

Where Breathing Changes

In the link between meaning and form,
says our poetry teacher, *content is always*
more important than form, but form
enhances meaning.

She also confirms my belief that a good
poet deviates from the meter for a good
reason, for a special meaning.
I'm in the right class.

My mind whisks me out of class
to prove her point.
I enter a space where breathing changes.
An edifice of discomfort pulls me in.
Rooms in this museum of memory of evil
and its evidence aren't square or plumb,
just off kilter enough to disorient, deceive
in the solemnity of the contents. The sun
rises on the wrong side, its adjacent
stream runs the wrong way.

My mind cannot yet return to class.
It stays in the DC Holocaust Museum
where structure goes organically wrong,
but not enough for the eccentricity of walls
and ceiling to be obvious to everyone.

It unsettles me…breaks…my…rhythm…apart
as I…ponder…the…message
its contents share.

Evie Groch

Laurie Hailey

Laurie Hailey is a retired English teacher who lives in Walnut Creek, California, and Oxford, New York. She has been writing poetry on and off for many years. Her poems have been published in the *Benicia Herald* and the Benicia Literary Arts anthology *Nooks and Crannies*. Laurie and three other poets, Johanna Ely, Mary Eichbauer, and Deborah Bachels Schmidt, have a collection of their poems published in their book, *Love's Meditation* (Random Lane Press, 2023).

Shape Shifting

Watch your mouth!

Lips pursed—

(Oh—
purple shape
of a sea anemone
without protective
stinging tentacles)

Lips stretch—

I'll wipe that smile off your face.

(Some sea anemones
split in two for self-protection)

Involuntary squint—

Don't you cut your eyes at me!

(But sea anemones
have no eyes)

Look at me when I'm talking to you!

Stone-faced respect—

(Sea anemones sway
with hypnotic motion)

You know this is for your own good.

Laurie Hailey

Remembering Maureen

My dear friend,
you have been gone eleven years,
and I welcome your subtle haunting.

Your specter slips into me,
into my gait, into the swing of my arms,
lumbering and large.

You're there in a melody,
the one I can't quite hum,
though I know it.

A whiff of jasmine,
or a hearty laugh
conjures a memory of the two of us,

and I look around
expecting to see your smile
before realizing that you are gone.

The impossibility of never seeing
you again scars—
little wounds that scab over time.

And as I age, it seems to me
that I walk in a daily
malaise of loss—

So, I welcome your haunting
when you cast
remembrance upon me,
my dear, Maureen.

Laurie Hailey

Leave me, please

Maybe I had you too long—
seventy years of mothering,
not that I would have wished
for the sorrow that others have known,
their mothers dead at seventy-three—heart attack,
dead at thirty-nine—liver cancer,
fifty-six—breast cancer
(now that gets a lot of them).

It's just that I can't stop writing about you,
and surely there are more interesting
topics than the death and loss of one's mother,
but I got so used to having you around
like the predictable way the seasons change,
there you were with your unsolicited advice,
your opinions providing some weird kind of consistency—

But now you are really gone,
and I am afloat, my silly toes dangling
from low-lying clouds. I can't seem to find the ground
because you're not here to pull me down, so I flounder.

Wine helps a little—
I see you through wet eyes,
almost hear your voice,
your laughter at my uncertainty—
and really how can I show the real me
who wants to lie down
and scream and scream and scream
Why did you leave me?
So, I guess I'll just keep writing
until you dissipate and fade away.

                                          Laurie Hailey

Kathleen Herrmann

Kathleen Herrmann writes poems about small moments with big feelings. A retired elementary educator, she taught writer's workshops to children, who, in turn, reawakened her inner child with their powers of observation and honesty. She has published nonfiction articles as well, on topics ranging from parenting skills to home security. She is currently interviewing refugees, compiling their stories for her new book, *I Was There, Now I'm Here*. Music is her twin passion. She currently sings in a local trio and plays piano, guitar and ukulele. Kathleen is the newly appointed Co-Poet Laureate for Vallejo, California.

The Day Lahaina Burned

August afternoon in paradise
Locals work, tourists play, windsurfers skip across the big blue
Pale gray smoke mars hilltop horizon
Charcoal clouds mushroom, race downhill, swirling embers ignite
Old Town
Where Kamehameha reigned, missionaries thundered, whalers
imbibed, Chinese laborers worshipped
Ancestral footprints erased

Dazed hotel guests wheel bags outdoors
Poolside loungers gape as flames lick rooftops
Frantic residents navigate side streets
Black cyclone, orange firewall hiss like monstrous blowtorch
Some bolt for the sea, others grip steering wheel
Blackout

First light exposes three square miles of gnarled wreckage,
mounded ashes, toppled washing machines
Cadaver dogs find bodies so fragile they fall apart
Coast Guard rescues traumatized survivors among floating corpses
Grizzled Banyan stands, charred canopy bereft of raucous mynahs
Understory not yet told
It stands

                                        Kathleen Herrmann

Hand of the Iguana

"It is not the strongest of the species nor the most intelligent that
survives, it is the one most adaptable to change."
      —attributed to Charles Darwin

Land iguana crosses dirt trail oblivious to human presence
Fingers and toes clutch, muscular arms hoist torso up and over
jagged rock
Slow steady pace slackens to a stop under sparse shade of cactus
Golden head turns, ancient eyes roam barren landscape

Marine iguanas sunbathe on slick lava rock, an inert tangle of
heads, tails, limbs
Snorts, snuffles and wheezes erupt into cattywampus display
Jets of expelled sea water shoot high above our heads
Each one arcs, raining down on leathery backs
One by one, spike-crested heads lift to the call of churning
azure seas

Hand of the iguana dangles from hefty arm covered in scaly amour
Tapered fingers tipped with sharp curved claws make soft skin
prickle
Macabre hand belies pacific herbivore, staying alive
Through drought, famine, birds of prey and human being
Staying alive

Kathleen Herrmann

Unwanted

July 1973
Protestors decry Roe v Wade on TV
I watch on vintage green couch next to Nana
I relish this time, this place
Lady slippers in the woods, cardinals at the feeder, unpinning
wilted wash in a sudden shower,
crunchy creamy bites of grilled cheese, even kneeling at
Sunday Mass
But abortion rights—I am certain I can read her mind

I lay the silver, baked beans simmer
I think it's a good law, she says
Our eyes meet
There's nothing worse than an unwanted child
One word fills her tiny kitchen, *unwanted*
There's nothing worse
I know how she knows
Baked bean pool blurs on my plate

June 2022
Protestors decry Roe v Wade, others fight to save it too late
Low-income families, single mothers, teens with consent,
10-year-old rape victim take the hit

Kathleen Herrmann

"Y'all wanna see the new Elvis movie?" grandgirl asks
between bites of buttermilk pancakes
"For sure."
We relish this time, this place
I wrap cool fingers around warm mug, our eyes meet
I have something important to tell you
I think it was a good law…

June 2023
25 million women have little or no choice
They travel far, pay more than they can afford, others live with
dire consequences
But voters say yes to choice every time
Red, blue and in between, we, the people say yes
May our voices prevail

Kathleen Herrmann

Christine Horner

She first knew Benicia as a sixth grader at the old St. Catherine's Academy when her Air Force father was stationed at Travis AFB. After an itinerant childhood common to military families, she returned to California for college at Stanford and UCSF nursing school, marriage and raising a family in Berkeley. She has since returned to live in the Reliez Valley back roads to Benicia. Her work has appeared in the CSPS *Poetry Letter and Literary Review*, NLAPW's *The Pen Woman*, and *Blue Unicorn*, and on-line at *Sugar Mule* and *Persimmon Tree*. Her book, *Stranger in the House, Selected Poems*, was published by dvs publishing, 2014. She continues to write various forms of poetry and studies traditional haiku with the Yuki Teikei Haiku Society.

Tell Me, Muse

So, through me, freedom and the sea
will call in answer to the shrouded heart.
        —Pablo Neruda, "The Poet's Obligation"

How will it be spilled,
how will it be poured out,
this dark honey too heavy
at the bottom of consciousness?

How will some leaven breathe
itself into the dough making light
by heady yeast of what
we may not want to know?

Will you wake the alien
visitor, sleeping within
or tap our deep divinities
to lead us through the gate
of gardens scented with orange?

Tease no more, Muse
lift us from this place of sunning
on blankets in quiet grass,
steel us to the work beyond words
that speaks for others, the assignment
to which Neruda invites us.

                    Christine Horner

Souvenir

Who is this child so lost,
this beggar child
who calls in my dream?
Did we walk once on strange sands
holding our shoes? Did he
want to hold my hand?
So forlorn, he pretends
to be independent. How dare I
pretend to care
about his spindly legs, open sores?
How do I remember
his round face, his darkened eyes?

We rode for a time in a rickshaw,
he in his rags and grime.
I fumbled with a few strange coins
asked, in darkened whispers,
"Who are you?" and without knowing

I brought him home,
this stowaway from a foreign beach,
he who brings me to tears waking,
stone-bruised through the soles
of midnight dreams.

Christine Horner

Kindred

I put my cheek against the mule's,
smell his smell, his sweat with mine.
I feel his prickled hairs
just at the curve of my jaw,
or is it his jaw? In tandem,
we two descend
into the belly of the canyon.

Now add the scent of old leather,
warm with the heat of our bodies—
this strap, that saddle, how
they lie against us, how they come
from some third animal, to us,
to the mule and me, until

together we feel the inevitable
thirst swallow us. Soon
the mule's feet are become mine
and fatigue a numbness even
to the slip of loose rocks.

                                                    Christine Horner

Georgette Howington

Georgette Howington's poems have been published in print and online journals such as *Iodine*, *Sleet*, and *The Poeming Pigeon*, among others. Her poetry has won awards at the North American Women's Music Festival, the Benicia Love Poetry Contest and Ina Coolbrith Circle Contests, and has also been published in local anthologies. She's a naturalist, gardener and conservationist living in the San Francisco Bay Area with her husband, Bruce, two cats and two goldfish!

Today I am Open to the Presence of Miracles

The world gives me a prayer list. One for refugees to
find safe homes, one to end wars, one to slow climate
disruption and help humans to make changes, one to
create awareness that animals are sentient and should
not be mistreated, one for the homeless, one for the
elderly who are alone, one for the forgotten mentally ill,
one for rain after three years of drought…

Today I saw a grasshopper on a leaf, paper wasps gliding on the birdbath,
a hummingbird perched on a tiny branch, a spider rushing
to its burrow in the grass, the cat sleeping by the window,
a fox running in the distance, Bushtits hungrily eating suet,
my hands making a cup of hot tea, grateful to God for the
frogs singing after a week of drenching rain.

                                                    Georgette Howington

Sonnet for Socks

Al and Barb served the homeless
every Saturday for twenty years.
News spread far; they came to rest.
Weary spirits, tragic, many tears
packages of kindness, acts of love.
A toothbrush, soap, socks and more.
Soiled hands, grateful they'd come
strangers touched them to their core.
One last man rushing arrived.
Packages gone, Al and Barb leaving.
He told them he'd walked for miles,
needed socks, feet sore, and bleeding.

Reaching out to this tired, deserving soul
Al took his socks off, "I have one more."

Georgette Howington

Unsettled While Washing Dishes

On the news today, I saw men and children bathing in the Mediterranean Sea, some pouring the salt water into five-gallon vessels to take home, women knelt on wet sand washing clothes in muddy basins as I ate my dinner of french lentil soup and chickpea flatbread. As I rinsed the dishes, I watched bits of food flush down the drain, my hands moving much like the women I saw in the news. Old woman hands. Ones that changed our babies' diapers, cooked hundreds of meals for our families, wiped the mouths of elderly parents, fitted the dresses for daughter brides, and gardened season after season for family vegetables. I don't feel guilty,or do I? It's not my fault. I did not start the war, nor did I throw any bombs, I have nothing against the Palestinians or the Jews in Israel. Hating the terrorists strikes me as something I should do but there's a part of me who can't hate anyone. Then again, maybe, if one cut my child's hands off, sliced my sister's breasts off and slaughtered my husband, I would. Hate. And hate with a fierce vengeance. Hate. I watch the fresh, clean water flush down the drain and I turn off the faucet. Who am I to have all this food, and choice of thought, and water I can drink? Who am I to be so blessed?

Georgette Howington

Joanne Jagoda

After retiring, one inspiring writing workshop launched Joanne Jagoda of Oakland on an unexpected writing trajectory. Her prize-winning short stories, poetry and creative nonfiction appear on-line and in numerous print anthologies, including *The Write Launch*, *Persimmon Tree*, *Burningword Literary Journal*, *Thirty West*, *Better After Fifty*, *Poetica*, *The Ravens Perch*, *Passager* and other publications. She received a Pushcart Prize nomination and has won a number of contests, including the Benicia Love Poetry contest. In 2022, Joanne received first place in the *Gemini* Open Poetry competition.

Writing helped her get through her breast cancer diagnosis. Her first book of poetry, *My Runaway Hourglass, Seventy Poems Celebrating Seventy Years,* was conceived during the pandemic (Poetica Publications, 2020). Jagoda has worked closely with several well-known poets. She continues taking Bay Area and national writing workshops, enjoys Zumba on line and spoiling her seven grandchildren.

The Tale of a Fat Ugly Crow
on a May Afternoon

In front of my living room window,
on a splendid, sunny May afternoon,
a fat crow rapturously caws over its good fortune.
I watch in morbid fascination
as it tears apart a rodent.
Can't fault the crow, a natural predator.
It studiously picks away at that small, hapless animal,
guts torn, splayed.
The next morning, not a morsel left,
not even a bloodstain, I checked the street.
Russia is tearing apart Ukraine without remorse,
destroying homes, churches, schools, hospitals,
disrupting millions, traumatizing the children,
injuring and killing civilians,
decimating infrastructure piece by piece,
ripping away the guts and sinew
of a once proud sovereign nation.
Soon it too will be left without a morsel
while the world watches from the window.

                                    Joanne Jagoda

Oh Sweet Summer

Oh lady summer, dear sweet girl,
we are trying to hold on to your skirts,
but you're in a big hurry
to take your leave.
Days getting shorter,
light receding, a retreating ocean wave;
grasses dry and brittle,
tired petals falling,
leaves brown and crackly.
Why can't we ask for an extension
like a late check out at the hotel?
How about a little more of your lazy days
the freedom of your beneficence
to help us forget in the warmth of your sunshine
all that's wrong around us, all we don't want to face:
hearings starting up again,
truth battered and spun,
rising prices, lying candidates,
homelessness and teacher shortages.
Fall and winter waiting in the wings…
what will the next months bring?
Mother nature's gentle scolding or harsh punishments,
wildfires or torrential rains,
flooding or no rain at all
to grace our thirsty, parched land.
Oh sweet summer, you will be sorely missed
in days of uncertainty to come.

Joanne Jagoda

Audacity

Why does life still feel like a wobbling Jenga game?
Pull out the wrong piece and it will all fall down.
Did I dare have the audacity to think
we would spring back to *Before Covid*,
return to *normal* with a wave of a magic wand?
As if all the canceled and postponed wedding receptions,
memorials, parties
stacked up like cars in a freeway traffic jam
would actually ever take place?
So many things not working, not the same.
Menus replaced by QR codes,
favorite restaurants shuttered;
My hair stylist left the area.
Book a flight, but your reservation might get canceled,
because there aren't enough pilots,
and you'll be stuck on hold for three hours trying to re-book
with oh so friendly customer service somewhere overseas
whom you can barely understand because of the poor connection
while roosters crow in the background.
And if you do fly, you'll play luggage *roulette*.
And the favorite place you've stayed in forever in the Napa Valley
has doubled its prices to make up for all the money they've lost.
And your gynecologist moved and didn't bother to tell you.
Covid keeps hanging around, like an obnoxious uncle
the one who has overstayed his welcome and smells like old cigars,
and farts.
I thought I was home-free with all my vaccinations and boosters,
until I got knocked down,
couldn't eat, couldn't taste,
left weak and vulnerable for weeks.

                                                    Joanne Jagoda

Slowly I climbed back up off the mat,
but my mojo was gone, my confidence ripped away.
Hesitant to go to plays, movies, concerts or out to dinner,
wondering about wearing masks again.
Normal? What was I even thinking?

Joanne Jagoda

Tanya Joyce

Tanya Joyce is a Bay Area poet and visual artist. On her first day in San Francisco, she ran into an old friend who introduced her to Beat poets Philip Whalen and Lew Welch. Tanya met a KJAZ DJ in front of City Lights Bookstore and studied drawing and writing with Manuel Neri, Wright Morris, and John Gardner. So why haven't you ever heard of Tanya Joyce? Because she has gone her own way and done her own thing—including making art her teachers didn't like. In spite of it all, Tanya has four books in print. Her poetry has won awards at the Dancing Poetry Festival, the Ina Coolbrith Circle, and The Poets Dinner. She chaired the Writers and Art Group at the San Francisco Women's City Club for nearly ten years and has designed costumes, flags, and banners for the Dancing Poetry Festival.

I Am Buddha

I am Buddha, the one with big ears.
I am short and fat, my eyes are open wide.
    From Persia to Japan, old tales of me persist.
You find me squinting where the wind is fierce.
My penciled mustache curves in style.
I am he or she.
I laugh at your gender distinctions.
And you laugh at mine.
Tongues wag—
Mine included.
    I'm not always handsome.
I'm not always young.
My shoulders droop sometimes.
My breasts sag
And my paunch sticks out.
    Don't believe what you hear
About my proportions.
    Don't believe that what you see
Holds all the truth.
Get up off the floor
With your bowing and scraping.
    If you kiss my feet
Make sure I've just washed them.
    The truth does not live in me.
Go outside and watch the day change.
Take a bus. Visit a museum.
Clean up rat droppings
And make friends with rats who left them.
Play music for oxen. Roar with a tiger.
Ask a rabbit for the elixir of immortality.
If you understand the rabbit's instructions
You have it.

                            Tanya Joyce

Willow Shoots

Willow shoots spring high
Above the stream bank.
The neighbors' front door
Is hardly visible.

Through the window
An elderly man is visible
Struggling to cross the room.

March, Duboce Park

It is spring.
Cats
Give up eating houseplants for
Fresh crabgrass
In the park.
Old women drink beer
By the retaining wall.
Men
Squint
Into the sun
And male dogs
Do not fight one another.
For women with babies
The time goes quickly.

Tanya Joyce

Prashant Kafle

Prashant Kafle, now living in Benicia, is from Nepal. His poems, in English, have appeared in the *Benicia Herald*.

Iron Dome

Who cares about roses in battle time?
A poor delicate flower
Who easily fades from small hail or straw
I need to plant now an iron dome in my yard
So I can defend against the enemy's missiles
Where at least I can protect my dad's grave
Where my mother buried him
Under his favorite Sugar Moon Rose.

We don't need telephone tower now
Because there is not any good news
to share with family and friends,
Here just need modern war weapons
F-16, Leopard tank, iron dome,
air strike warning system in my city,
so at least we can protect poor cat "Melly"
and obedient companion dog "Jelly"
Because these innocent animals don't deserve
to die in humans' meaningless, egoist fight.

I don't have any wish more than this,
If God exists somewhere in the universe,
Please don't separate my sister from me...

Prashant Kafle

Shy Plant

You woke up in the morning
  with sun's first rays landed
  on your forehead.
I was standing next to you
  Just behind the marigold
  I saw your opening eyes as
    rose petal
You were holding the entire
  blue ocean there from whole
  night which you collected sparkle
  dew drops inside the depth
  of your dreams
  and you were trying to fly
  as pigeon's cheeks who just
  grow all feathers in their wings
  under the surveillance of
    mother's shadow
Now time walks so fast
Now the sun almost
    arrives on the horizon,
I just hear the sound
    of rain and I saw your
    hair is full of snowfall.

I wanted to talk more
  at your precious smile
  with sun but I think
  it's time to go to bed my love,
Just hug me silently
    under the full moon
    inside your closing fingers
Just like a shy plant at midnight
  in the countryside.

Prashant Kafle

Monkey's Metaphor

Love is like a carnivorous
  plant.
It has beauty
It has nectar
It is surrounded by sweet
  dream's pitchers

All lovers want to fall in it
  Like the way a bucket
  wants to fall in a well
But only the lucky gets back
  in life
Most fall as the rocks from
  a cliff
  which never yet get back in the
  same place
Love is like Nepenthe
  it has attractive diamond drops
But it raises a unique
  death crop.
Shakespeare may be laughing
  to see my monkey metaphors
  to love
    beyond his Red Red Rose.

                    Prashant Kafle

Sandy King

Sandy King was born and raised in the San Francisco Bay Area too many years ago to remember. She has always liked being outdoors instead of indoors. Sandy and her family spent many summers visiting western states' National Parks. The family's favorite was Yosemite where they went every single year.

Sandy graduated from UC Berkeley, first receiving her bachelor's degree in history and then in the following year, her California Teacher Credential. She taught Elementary School as well as Middle School. In 1997 she received her Master of Arts with honors in Education Administration at Saint Mary's College in Moraga, California.

Now retired, she spends her time in her garden, hiking in the Sierra Nevada Mountains, spoiling her two beloved Dalmatians, and writing poetry and short stories. Her writing is most often about the wonders of nature, especially the animals. Many of her poems have been published in *The Avocet* as well as in local poetry publications.

A Gentle Arrival, a villanelle

Change is coming in the air,
longer days and shorter nights.
Dogwoods will blossom, now they're bare.

Snow mounds dripping here and there,
in due time creeks will swell from melting ice.
Change is coming in the air.

Raccoons seek food they do not share,
courting owls call for mates each night.
Dogwoods will blossom, now they're bare.

Mama bears with newborn cubs sleep unaware
the cold season is waning every night.
Change is coming in the air.

In the snow, paw prints of a snowshoe hare,
nearby a coyote licks his chops under moonlight.
Soon dogwoods will blossom, now still bare.

A gentle breeze whispers change is in the air,
an osprey pair begins nest building at first light.
Long-awaited, Spring arrives without fanfare.
Now dogwoods blossom, no longer bare.

Sandy King

Garden Orb Weaver, a villanelle

A garden spider weaves in my backyard
She is building her web—a work of art
Spinning her silver strands across the yard

Winter's cold winds blow without regard
To the small brown spider's determined heart
Garden spider weaves in my backyard

She spins through the day, the work is hard
Continuing to spin, she won't depart
Spinning her silver strands across the yard

What does she think as she weaves and darns
As blustery winds tear her web apart
Spider still weaving in my backyard

Light dwindles, now the time of moon and stars
Almost done she works alone in the dark
Spinning her silver strands across the yard

In the morning she's in her web on guard
A fly, first meal caught in her web, a good start
My garden spider weaves in my backyard
Spinning her silver strands across the yard

Sandy King

Waiting For Springtime

For months I have hibernated inside my cabin.
Plenty of time to nap, read new books, cook hearty soups.
The wood stove is warming the house day and night.
I've enjoyed the gentle snowfalls of winter.

Days when gray clouds are blown away.
When weak sunlight shows its presence,
I walk in the nearby forest looking for signs
Winter's time is waning.

My pace keeps me warm in the still chilly air.
Sniffing the forest air, I am treated to
the moist, loamy, fragrance of the soil and plants
recently covered by snow.

Dogwood trees are starting to show signs
of new green leaves on the way.
Looking up, I see ponderosa pines with
tiny pinecones peeking back at me.

Hibernating animals will awaken soon.
Canada geese, blacktail deer, and other
migrating beasts will return with the equinox.
For now, gray squirrels dig in the soil seeking
their Fall acorn stashes.

 I return home with mixed feelings.
Though Winter's slow pace is delightful,
I am ready for next season: the warming,
colorful, noisy, return of Spring in all her glory.

Sandy King

D.L. Lang

Vallejo Poet Laureate Emerita D.L. Lang is an internationally published poet whose work appears in over 60 anthologies worldwide. A winner of the 2023 Curbside Haiku contest, her haiku was displayed across downtown Tulsa, Oklahoma, and archived at the Woody Guthrie Center. She has performed her poetry hundreds of times at festivals, demonstrations, and literary events across California. In 2023 she performed at the Woody Guthrie Folk Festival at the History Center in Okemah, Oklahoma, as one of the Woody Guthrie Poets accompanied by David Amram on piano and standing on a replica of Woody's front porch. Her poems have been transformed into songs, used as liturgy, and to advocate for a better world. She has received proclamations from the California State Senate, California Arts Council, and Vallejo City Council for her poetic contributions and service as poet laureate. She is a member of the Revolutionary Poets Brigade.

Angel Cities

Our mantra was movement, and movement was joy.
Ripped away from routine, there is room to dream.
Memories come rushing back in the stillness
with the exploration of inner and outer worlds.

The map lures us in with its questions,
begging us to wander infinite routes.
Roving gangs of pigeons encircle the sky—
soaring silhouettes around a blazing sun.

We wept at the graves of legends.
Immortality may be etched in vinyl,
but magic moments still slip away.
When will they build a time machine?

We took a ramble in the canyon,
shopping at the country store,
talking about the musicians
who earned their laurels in these hills.

LA—where the call of the ocean
meets the end of the mother road,
where angels and stars mingle in a galaxy,
and palm trees tower towards infinity.

Traffic like molasses takes an eternity.
It would take decades to see all there is to see.
I'd rather take another walk down Venice Beach,
smiling back at sun baked seagulls hovering over me.

D.L. Lang

Unbalanced Budget

The U.S. wants to shut down the government
because they can't balance a budget.
They want to close 400 national parks
and furlough the workers who maintain them
even though the national parks bring in funds.

I have a better idea. Look at what costs the most.
They spend more on war than everything else combined.
How about they stop building new war machines:
the tanks, bombs, warplanes, nukes, and guns?

The U.S. spends more on war than any other country.
How about they stop attacking our international neighbors,
which only leaves innocent people and cities in ruins?

Maybe then we'd have enough tax dollars
to support infrastructure, the post office, welfare,
education, social security, healthcare,
and not have to close a single national park.

This country's addiction to destruction
is destroying the world, polluting the planet,
murdering millions, and it's high time to stop it.
We'd all be better off funding national parks
than building another murderous rocket.

D.L. Lang

Who Put Catnip in my Coffee?

Who put catnip in my coffee?
What herbs were in this tea?
Honeysuckle? Valerian?
Perhaps, some silver vine?

We're all slowly growing whiskers,
sprouting tails and glowing eyes.
Whatever's in this brew feels a bit feline.

Looking out in awe upon this wild scene.
Enveloped by a living rainbow,
faces purple, orange, and green—
this party is the cat's meow.
It's like none you've ever seen.

Alley cats give speeches
that we all can understand
as if there was no boundary
between feline and humanity.

Thunderous applause
emanates from kitten claws
as we meow in harmony.

A wise old house cat croons
her entire autobiography.
At the end of reincarnation,
her nine life cycle almost complete,
she said that being loved
was life's true immortality.

D.L. Lang

Ramona Lappier

Born and raised in Minnesota, Ramona Lappier* is a poet who, via Hawaii and Washington, has lived for nearly 40 years in northern California. She is grateful for the inspiration and encouragement of Benicia's First Tuesday Poets' group who have made her feel welcome since 2018. Her poems debuted in the *Benicia Herald* column, "Going the Distance," and have been published in two Benicia Literary Arts anthologies.

Ramona, aka "Mona," "Monie," and "Mo," is the mom of two sons and the "Grandma Monie" of three grandchildren with whom there is never enough time.

(*Rhymes with "appear")

Made in America—The Weapons Fetish

Made in America, the weapons fetish
is an infection across the land.
All the rabid mutts come a'runnin' to the whistle.
Little bitches bite down to bear the brand.

That gun doesn't grow your dick, little boy.
That gun doesn't make you a big man.
That gun doesn't make you right, just self-righteous.
That gun is toxic anger in your hand.

The Second Amendment doesn't say it's okay
to shoot Grandma and kill kids at school.
But asshats like Texas' Governor Abbott
damn the innocents to defend the killing tool.

So sacred is the gun when one is hungry to rule.
And greed is the seed in that garden of cruel.

Common sense is undone
by well-funded fools
who blame mental health,
blame the doors on the school
where the children perished,
where their blood made pools,
seemingly bottomless,
crimson pools
fed by the gun,
cherry red pools
lives torn asunder,
scarlet pools
ruby red pools
ruddy, bloody pools
where the children perished,
and the fucking weapon won.

                                              Ramona Lappier

I Oughta Go T' Minnesota

I oughta go t' Minnesota
to dance in knee-deep snow
beneath the phosphorescent green
aurora borealis glow.

There is shimmer above and shiver below
10,000 lakes. I really oughta go,
to wander, not lost,
in the shadows of birches
that fall like an
unwritten score
lining the
virgin white page
of the forest.
My footprints form notes
on the floor,
an unfolding story
told as it plays,
as I wander, not lost,
on a cold winter day.
I'm there in the mist
where memories stay,
there, where I was born.

And here, in California,
measures counted in years,
joyful crescendos, tremolos of tears,
I come to the coda with mezzo forte fear.

So, ya know,
I oughta go t' Minnesota
to dance in knee-deep snow
beneath the phosphorescent green
aurora borealis glow.

Ramona Lappier

Son
January, 2022

Thirty six years
loving you.
Five years
missing your face,
though every day,
always,
I think of you.
I think I see you
all over the place.

I thought I saw you once
in the grocery store,
your back to me
in the produce aisle.
You turned,
face masked,
and it hurt
I couldn't be certain…
it's been such
a very long while.

Happy 36th birthday, son.
I miss the light of your smile.

This distance imposed
can be closed, son,
if only hearts will allow,
though know, in due time,
I will go, son.
All we truly have is Now.

I love you dearly,
Mom

                                        Ramona Lappier

Ronna Leon

Ronna Leon served as Benicia's third Poet Laureate. She thinks of poets laureate as citizen poets. She and her husband have lived in the city since 1983 where they raised three of their children. She currently is the Printmaking Program Coordinator for Arts Benicia, arranging for classes and running the Printmakers Workshop for the past 11 years.

Rapping at My Door

The photo of my Granddaughter
dressed for Halloween as DEATH:
(long black robe, and plastic scythe)
came this morning.
Her little brother as a skeleton clings to her side.
HAPPY Halloween.
I'm told she did the makeup herself:
pale faces with blackened eyes and lines across
her brother's mouth to indicate stitches.
He doesn't smile but she half grins.
They hold an orange and a turquoise bucket.
Pay up or else.

Having spent the last year avoiding this specter
and knowing that thus far
over five million have failed world wide
because of one tiny virus,
I'm still plenty scared.
And uneasy seeing this brave child
take the role.
Death doesn't do irony.

Ronna Leon

Holding Hands

Babies are offered fingers to grasp.
Toddlers told "hold my hand" at intersections.
Children race down the street, fingers interlaced.
Lovers hold hands well into old age.
When visiting the sick, it's the gesture of compassion.

Holding hands creates a bond,
a bridge of understanding: we are not alone.
Simple, beautiful.

On 9–11 when people jumped from the towers
some held hands.

When an angel asks you to hold their hand
or you are moved to tell one, "please hold mine"
try to keep it simple,
just the ordinary truth of relationship,
trust.

Don't worry about where you're going,
don't fret.
Savor that particular touch.
Be the child we all are.
That is miracle enough.

In response to Nikki Basch Davis' "I've Got You" Sculpture

Ronna Leon

By Definition

The night settles a house, fills the rooms with a still quiet
like hesitation, like waiting, like loneliness, like a bitterness.

Turn on lights and night recedes, presses against the window,
crowds the dark closet and cupboard, hunkers down on the landing
bides its time, a blanket that won't be thrown off until morning.

Night has substance, has its own way of illuminating—
glimpsed in dreams, whispered on winds, plays with memory,
shadows throwing more shadows, the endless mirror reflecting
into eternity, a vertigo of doubt and ambivalence.

Struggle, it makes no difference. Night catches, clings
blooms to universal, becomes relentless reality,
engulfing us all. Settle down. Sleep. Forget. Try to.
Morning may come. Repeat. Night again,
claiming every fantasy.

                                                          Ronna Leon

Karen Marker

Karen Marker is an Oakland-based poet and memoirist whose work draws on her family roots and branches in places that include New Orleans, Sweden, New England, Ohio and Vilna. She also turns to her studies in psychology, classical mythology, and religion for inspiration. Her work has recently been published in *The MacGuffin*, won awards through the Ina Coolbrith Circle and been included in the Kent State University May 4th Archives. A chapbook will be coming out in the next year with Finishing Line Press.

Red Fox

The night when you come
like spring's first breath
to my back door I am speechless.

Our eyes lock. For seconds
time stops. What do I call you?

The full pink moon reflects upon
your silver fur as you search for
what I hide inside.

When you turn away you wave
a wide flag tail. I remember the world
I'd lost. The word that is your name.

Tomorrow I will follow your soft footsteps
through the green hills above the city. California
poppies will burst diaphanous among bright
yellow mustard. Coral bells, purple iris,

a baby snake just hatched will appear
on the path with everything else that hungers,
full of hope, still wild and unnamed.

                                               Karen Marker

When the Divorce Happens

After the painting, "The Two Frida's," by Frida Kahlo, 1939

"I am my own muse, the subject I know best, the subject I want to know better." — Frida Kahlo

She wakes in a storm
dream, her body's
worn, not broken but turned
into two, heavy clouds
have gathered. Now she is
they with one heart
opened. Fresh blood drips
down along the white
of a formal dress
into fallen leaves. The cold
scissors are still in one hand.
The other heart's extracted,
closed, out of the chest
on a blue and gold blouse,
at the end of a long bare neck.
Each one of their hearts is tied
to the other still pumping
through pain, arteries, veins,
all the threads connected,
the two of them wholly together,
They are fierce containment,
shut lips, four watchful
eyes. Hand on hand.
And him? Just a small
photograph cut out,
now gone. No cord
to life, no muse.

Karen Marker

I Couldn't Remember My Dream

I know that things were being sorted out.
One word, then another
leading into the epic work
of my life, my masterpiece
because I'd found the perfect
word for happiness, for peace
just at that moment when I woke.
Then I can't remember
what happens next.
I only know that in the morning light
something shattered.
The screen went blank.
My head exploded.
The pages were lost
and I was left excavating
the damage, all of it sand
without footprints. Under the sky
fringed with fast moving storm
clouds, flocks of birds flying south,
I couldn't find the beginning.
The only thing left was this ending—
war on the horizon.

Karen Marker

Juanita J. Martin

Juanita J. Martin, first Poet Laureate of Fairfield, California, is author of *The Lighthouse Beckons* and *Quiet Intensity* poetry books. She has poems in *Rattlesnake Review*, *Soma Literary Review*, *Blue Collar Review* and others. She also writes flash fiction, nonfiction articles, essays and book reviews. Her awards include a California Senior Poet Laureate Finalist Award—2012, and Honor Scroll Award—2011.

Juanita has been a member of California Writers Club—Redwood, Napa Valley, and Mount Diablo branch. She was managing editor of Napa Valley Writers' *Third Harvest 2021* anthology, where she published her first memoir, first flash fiction story, and poetry book reviews. Also in 2021, Juanita attended the Napa Writers Conference, studying poetry under Gillian Conley.

In 2023, Martin received Honorable Mention in the Benicia Love Poetry Contest for her poem "Love Haiku." She also received a Reserve Best of Show Ribbon for her poem "Before Covid-19," published in the *Benicia Herald* in 2020.

California's Thirst

As the sun burns the atmosphere
there's nowhere to quench our thirst
We envy dew on the flowers,
fog floating through the trees

Our state is dry again
With no viable resources left
Rationing is a way of life
Yet we're told it's not enough

The cracks are not from a 5.0
On the Richter Scale
The ground has puckered
From the lack of moisture

Dust-weary, we pray for relief
Gray clouds tease with scant showers
We are lap dogs underneath
With our tongues still panting

                              Juanita J. Martin

Where I Find Peace

In the humor of living
gentle strokes of animal fur
crevices of art, nature and song,
splashes of color and light
tug of wind in my hair
a moonlit caress
rippled waves along the shore
the whisper of snow
A rainwater dance
A sunlit smile
Falling asleep to crackling embers
love in the form of a sigh
Innocence at play
trickle of sand between my toes
nimble fingers on my back
As cloud-pillows collide
in an azure sky
Heaven awakes to a watchful eye
this woman on her knees
burdens stay beneath my loads

Juanita J. Martin

If People Were Flowers

If people were flowers
in luxurious earth
They'd feverishly dance
Open themselves to an innocuous sun

If people were flowers
They'd travel winds of opportunity
Nestle in babbling brooks,
Mind and body naked and carefree

If people were flowers
They'd raise their designer heads
Feast upon imagination
in gardens of blinding light

If people were flowers
They'd hold pristine petals of love
spread bouquets of color
uplift every soul around the world.

Juanita J. Martin

Louise Moises

Louise Moises was born and raised in Redwood City, California, and is now a resident of Richmond, California. She began writing poetry in 2017 as a means of dealing with grief. Her vision has since expanded to include a wide range of subjects, including adventures and stories drawn from her solo RV trips across the country. She especially enjoys performing her poems at gatherings in person and on Zoom. Her poems have been recognized by the Ina Coolbrith Circle, Artists Embassy International, Voices of Lincoln, and local county fairs. She has been published in a variety of anthologies, including *California Poetry Society*, *Wingless Dreamer*, *A Gathering*, *Unlimited Literature*, *The Avocet*, et al. She feels blessed by the friendship and encouragement of many poets.

Balcony View

From my balcony I can look down at the road,
a way of passing the time,
I read, write, glance down at the road.

The road leads into and out of Prescott, Arizona,
a high desert town of around 45,000 people,
nested like an eagle atop sandstone formations.
Known for its mild winters, when Knob Peak,
a landmark above the town sports a jaunty white cap.
In summer, a refuge for those escaping
the brutal heat of Phoenix, refuge also
for the rehabilitating: teen drug addicts,
middle class alcoholics, veterans with PTSD.

At over 5000 feet in elevation,
a training ground for every kind of athlete,
a favorite haunt of extreme bicyclists,
a tough ride up and down the mountain.
I see them daily from my balcony,
negotiating the winding road,
as they pass the sign *Share the Road*.

Three years ago, on a bright afternoon,
I watched a motorist miscalculate distance.
In a moment of suspended time, the bicyclist
flew into the air, bounced off the roof of the car,
crashed to the ground.
I reached for my phone, dialed 911,
ran downstairs with an armload of towels.
The victim helicoptered to a hospital in Phoenix.

Today, from my balcony,
I see a gathering of bicyclists,
the annual memorial ride.

                                    Louise Moises

The Egret

Silently stalks in the marshy mass
yellow legs lift stiffly from the knee,
feet land carefully in the hush,
eyes alert watching, waiting, neck extended.
Lacking a camouflage, the bird stands unmoving,
whiteness exposed against earth and sky.

I've come to this isolated spot
in search of answers to the why
of life and death and endless longing.
I find an unexpected companion in the egret,
who with purpose pauses.

I stand in quiet observation,
not wishing to disturb this communion.
The egret does not ask what day or month or year,
he knows only to hunt, to survive,
holds no judgement or belief,
no reason for emotion or devotion.

The egret takes a cautious step,
eye concentrating on the prize.
He darts, snaps, head rises
to reveal a silvery fish
caught tightly in the deadly beak.
The egret lifts his head, swallows whole.

A scene of life and death without a hero.
There is no mourning on the marsh.

Louise Moises

Blocks, Blueberries and Muddy Hands

A dozen wooden blocks clatter to the floor,
he's knocked them down for the tenth time,
maybe more. Together, we rebuild,
stack, count, balance.
His face glows with anticipation
for the moment of destruction.
Toy bulldozer rams the fragile pyramid.
He jumps up and down, bubbles with laughter.

Bored with blocks, he digs into the toy box
for musical instruments, toots a horn, bangs a drum,
hammers a xylophone. *Dance grandma*, he says.
I spin around the living room. *Faster*, he says.
At lunchtime, he refuses to eat.
We put blueberry eyes on slices of pizza,
make monkey faces with bananas and grapes.
He eats everything; asks for a reward.

After lunch, he shows me piles of leaf mold,
home to the biggest fattest worms.
We dig them up, transfer them
to the compost bin, watch them wiggle.
Next he runs in circles, leaps over stumps,
rolls on the sweet smelling grass of summer.
He digs a hole, calls it a construction zone,
fills it with water from the wading pool.

Louise Moises

He grins, threatens me with muddy hands.
I run away from him, shake with mock fear.
He jumps to his feet, chases me around
the yard, squealing with delight.
He is faster and more agile than me,
it's easy to let myself be caught.
He grabs me around the waist and shouts,
    I love you, Dancing Grandma!

Honorable Mention, 2023 Benicia Love Poetry Contest

Louise Moises

Katrina Monroe

Katrina (Kathy) Monroe is an East Coast transplant, loving her adopted town of Benicia! Her chapbook, *Transitions and Reinventions*, chronicles in poetry her first year here, from saying goodbye to places and people, to her heartfelt adventures all over California. She is currently working on two other chapbooks.

A retired therapist, she has a BA from Boston University in Sociology, an M.Ed. from Harvard in Counseling, and an MSW from Rutgers in Clinical Social Work, with nary a course in poetry. Instead, she has learned over the years from others' writings, presentations and workshops. Her "works of heart" have picked up some awards and publishing offers. When not writing or reading poetry, she fills her time volunteering with Carquinez Village, adventuring near and far in her RV, playing Trivia with Yacht Club teams, dancing at Jazzercise and with flash mobs, and walking her dog Rocky all over downtown. Katrina is Benicia's ninth Poet Laureate.

Haiku Septet for Yosemite

Half Dome of granite
turns hard face to morning light
daring the climber

Misty waterfalls
roar their power on descent
breaking the stillness

Ribbons of rivers
burble, tumble in their rush
over drifted rocks

Hiding deep secrets
Mirror Lake captures the sky
holds the universe

Native hiking trails
unveil valley mystery
baring its birthmarks

Ancient groves of trees
provide oxygen, beauty,
inspire tired nomads

Meadows of flowers
singing a swaddling refrain
"Come child, fall on me"

Katrina Monroe

To a Woman Named Ivana in Ukraine

Kindred Spirit

Sister, 7000 miles away,
hugging your husband good-bye in an unsafe home town
carrying your child down a rocket scarred road
jammed in a train jostling with others in joint sorrow
waiting like an animal to be
processed, inspected, admitted, housed, fed
wandering like a nomad to find a place of rest
I struggle to even imagine…
I, in a safe space, a warm embrace, a life of grace…
How can I grasp the depth of your pain?
But I am a wife, a mother, a woman, a human…
In my prayers and petitions,
in my limited powers of persistence,
I join my heart to yours.

Katrina Monroe

Quietude

Before
waves crash on the shore
whoosh forward over the sands,
retreat to the marimba sound
of a thousand pebbles sliding back into ocean…
there is in deep water an abiding
of continuous silent movement,
hushed above and below the surface,
a place where a boat can bob gently,
rocking itself in the reticence of the sea.

Before
night's strong winds hit the mountainside
tossing the treetops like laundry on a line,
when each timber's leaves sound their voices,
leading to a crescendo of notes throughout the hills…
there is the quiet of late evening,
trees sleep in the silence,
birds retreat to their nest,
crickets finally take their rest,
a camper can lie in his tent and hear his breath.

Before
clock's shrill alarm announces the morning,
fast talking journalists recite the news,
car engines roar down the road,
construction crews pound their pilings…
there is peace in the midnight hour,
technology interruptions are silenced,
darkness allows the mind to wander freely,
thoughts quietly spill onto paper,
so a poem can be peacefully birthed.

Katrina Monroe

Don Peery

Fourth Benicia Poet Laureate after original Poet Laureate, Joel Fallon. Proud compiler of *The Book of Joel*, being a look at Joel's life and wit as told through his poems. And then there was COVID. Less than a week after his second COVID shot, he suffered a stroke impacting the left side of his body and his speech. In recovery, he reads a lot but doesn't write much anymore. These three poems were his last, marking a turning point in his life…

2-9-2020

Nine months ago
I met the new, true love of my life.
My Lady, the one I had been with
the past fifteen years, saw it coming—
she's perceptive that way
having had a lot of experience,
good and bad,
before we got together.

When I went away and didn't come back
she told her family that we
were "in transition"
and not to expect to see me all that often
in spite of being there at the birth
of three of her four grandchildren
and me being Papa Don
to her Granny Mum.

But I couldn't help it—
my heart melting at first sight
of my new love's eyes,
her pouty mouth and flawless skin.
And now, the way she holds my hand
when we are close together and how,
when serenading her with song,
she reaches her fingers to gently touch my lips.

I am committed, consumed,
head over heels with a love that grows
each morning when she wakes smiling,
trusting me to begin her day
in warmth and comfort.
Holding her, I know,
that at nine months old,
I am hers…completely.

Don Peery

Love, In the Time of COVID

There is always a bit of sadness
        at the end of a good thing—

like saying goodbye to friends
at graduation;

or the last bit of candy
left over from Halloween;

or the last slice of pumpkin pie
at Thanksgiving;

or the last Port of Call
at the end of a cruise;

or the last beer in an Irish pub
before returning Stateside—

like the end of a relationship
inconvenient in a world-wide Pandemic,

driving home… teary eyed…
        remembering…

Funerals, I think,
are easier to bear.

Don Peery

11-8-2020
The Morning After

Sitting in the sun on the porch
in the crisp air of fall
—coffee in hand—
at ease with the world
on the morning after ending
a long-term affair,
I am content.

As the song says, "regrets,
I've had a few—but then again,
too few to mention." I've had
love enough to sustain me,
children to be proud of,
friends along the way
to keep me grounded.

With eighty years of history
to guide me—looking forward
to an end approaching—
a few things left to do
but nothing, in retrospect,
that I can say
is all that important.

And so I sit,
writing thoughts
to get my life in order—
tidying up,
keeping only what's essential,
letting go of what is not,
retaining hope, retaining life,
retaining love.

                                     Don Peery

Lois Requist

For years, Lois has been involved in the literary life of Benicia and the surrounding area. She writes and publishes poetry, fiction, nonfiction, and newspaper columns in the *Benicia Herald* for Carquinez Village. The three books she's written are *Where Lilacs Bloom*; *RVing Solo Across America, without a cat, dog, man, or gun*; and *Late Harvest Green*. She's currently working on a memoir, *Leaving the Faith of Our Fathers*.

As president of Benicia Literary Arts, Lois works to help other writers improve their writing and do what they want to do with it—publish, share, or just own it. As a previous Poet Laureate of Benicia, she mostly practices this kind of writing alone. She's been in a memoir group for many years, and states that "This has helped me in so many ways! I'm fortunate to live in this town."

A Dry Leaf

Picking up a rolled newspaper
Slapping it against my leg
Like Mother did, standing in that Idaho day
Autumn surrounding her, dry leaves
That once flew high at her feet

Memories surround me like old friends
Something to hold on to
At eighty, more past resides with me
Than present or future
As debris or treasure
Regret or delight

Mistakes mix with melodies
From passion too intense to burn for long
And the boys, my sons,
Swirl small at my feet, needing this or that
Today they tower above me, self sustaining

Where does the dry leaf go from here?
Crushed, burned, guttered, or blown away
Carried by the wind to a new and unimagined
Place or perhaps it never lands
Simply carried on the wind
Into the blue forever

Hints of the past
Following, sustaining the lift
Ever higher

                                         Lois Requist

Paradise Lost

On the ridgeline
black-silhouetted firemen
confront a raging hell

Not holy words
about fire and brimstone
the Campfire will not burn forever
long enough
unspeakable pain
utters volumes
this will not go away soon

Gone
all we planned for, saved
each paycheck sending dollars
to the bank, for the taxes
for a place of our own.
The graceful-spouted blue teapot
from grandmother
no one's now.
The bed where we slept
loved, curled into each other,
a shield made of ourselves.

We ran
against a wall of fire
some of us escaped
that day
when Paradise was lost

Paradise, California, is a small community almost totally burned in a wildfire in 2018, 85 dead.

Lois Requist

Sounds and Shadows

Walking in the beginning of day,
reveling in common sights and sounds,
a pug trots along by his man, a biker wheels by.

The breeze is languid on my lips
While flowers show up in crimson,
sky blue, white, and mustard.

Through walls a radio drones
a child's chipper voice
I can taste the corn flakes
see the soggy bottom of the bowl.

I can almost forget someone powerful
Is racing to make less of me,
Gender equality a past dream.

Health care for all forgotten,
women will again be denied.
Small but weighty men and women
Using their power to take away ours.

Almost, the morning silence smothers the inside scream
of women who for centuries have fought for equality.

The promise slipping away with the end of summer,
and the death of Ruth Bader Ginsburg
like the annuals that go away.
We thought we were planting perennials
even oak trees or redwoods.

                                    Lois Requist

Jane Russell

Jane lives in Pittsburg, California, with her two beautiful cats and her partner, Petey. She is a retired teacher, school counselor, college instructor and Marriage Family Therapist (MFT). Being a long time Sierra Club member and avid traveler, she especially enjoys writing poems about places she has visited and her experiences with nature and her environment. She belongs to a creative writing critique circle and is also a member of the San Francisco Bay Area Ina Coolbrith Circle. Some of her poems have been published in *The Avocet—A Journal of Nature Poetry*, *Suisun Valley Review*—Spring 2023 edition, and *Vistas and Byways Review*—S.F. State OLLI Fall 2023 edition. Besides writing poetry, she also enjoys music, especially folk music. Jane plays the guitar and mountain dulcimer and sings with the Threshold Choir, an *a capella* women's singing group.

Time Travels

Time is a continuum,
past a memory, future a mystery.
I'm holding on to the now,
for it is all I have at the moment.
Soon it will be gone
Like the blink of an eye,
Heart beat, tick of the clock.
It's elusive, moves softly on cat paws,
silent flutter of butterfly wings.
It is unseen except in footprints it leaves,
like paw tracks that melt in the snow,
or changes from bud to wither of flowers,
loved ones as they age.
It brings about destruction, death, decay,
also birth, healing, rebuilding and hope.

With time come cycles
of metamorphosis, birth to death,
animal migrations, seasonal changes.
I am in a progression of time and change.
When young, time seemed forever,
contained unlimited possibilities.
Now I am an elder,
Snapshots of my life move quickly,
Like an old time movie, fast forward.
There is a reality of limitation,
long term goals changing to short term,
procrastination to immediacy,
viewing each day as a gift of time.
Time is fleeting like a lithe gazelle.
Time, oh time, where did you go?

                                    Jane Russell

Trust in the Universe

This is my prayer to the Universe.
  May I remember that what I want
is not always in my best interest,
  the Universe can be wiser.
May I have belief in my ability
  to deal with adversities.
May I develop positive attitudes about outcomes,
  even though they may not be as I envisioned.
May I know that help and support
  can come from unexpected sources.
I'm never alone in my struggles.
  May I face challenges as a test,
builder of inner strength.
  May I have the vision to see
Silver linings in clouds.
  May I remember past challenges
which I have made it through.

May I understand that life is a landscape,
  rivers to cross, never a flat land.
Through the darkness there is always hope
  for brighter times ahead.
Fear of the unknown can be replaced
  with curiosity about things to come.
May I ask with anticipation,
  "What's next in my journey,"
knowing that surprises lie ahead.

May I spread my arms,
  let wind whip through my hair,
carry me to heights and depths,
  believing life is an adventure,
does not have a script.

Jane Russell

Whatever happens is my unique story.
Then may I play out my destiny,
   weather the storm,
be a wave surfer,
   coast in calm waters.

Wandering in a Strange Place

Why am I here in this place,
where taken by imagination,
I find myself wandering?
Things are as they should be.
Right is right, wrong is wrong.
Justice prevails, kindness abounds.
Truth is applauded, lies are forbidden.
This is a rainbow place
where sun shines many hues,
all shades and colors appreciated.

While dancing through fields of wildflowers,
green grass caresses my legs,
sweet fragrance of blossoms
fills my senses, calming my every pore.
Soft music flows, surrounds me,
embraces me in loving arms.
I feel secure, safe, everything predictable.
All beings are well, at peace,
no lurking darkness,
only warmth of sunlight.

Although I am a stranger,
I embrace this world,
a place of possibilities and hope.
Travels of my mind can take me here.
If it can be imagined, it can be.

                                        Jane Russell

Alyza Lee Salomon

Alyza Lee Salomon has worked as an editor and educator. Now blissfully retired, she continues to write poetry, dance, edit—and finally is in the process of completing several book projects. She ascribes her love of words and languages to a trilingual childhood with a European heritage, as filtered through the experience of growing up as a first-generation American. Her poems have appeared in local anthologies, and two essays on Virginia Woolf in scholarly journals. As a dancer, she has performed with Natica Angilly's Poetic Dance Theater Company since 2003. Alyza studied at Harpur College (now Binghamton U) and earned her master's degree in English Literature at Sonoma State University. She has lived in Maryland, upstate New York, and now for many years enjoys the natural wonders and cultural diversity of the San Francisco Bay Area.

A Flavor Called Delight

(on an artwork by Pat Calabro)

> Color and Line
> jump at the chance
> to dance divinely
>
> embracing space
> and racing time
> we jam and jive
>
> practicing the splash
> and the swirl,
> we unfurl
>
> not for rhyme
> but for rhythm
> and design:
>
> a purple heart
> or a blue ribbon
> can't compete
>
> with this jazzy
> dive into live
> joy sublime!

This poem appeared on the "Poet of the Month" page of the United Poets Laureate International website in December 2022.

Alyza Lee Salomon

Dusk on the Road to Tai'an

The sun's become a falling peach,
ripeness momentarily embraced
by delicate limbs of green saplings.

Proudly worshipping precious daylight,
these sweet young trees,
planted with mathematical regularity

by legions of lithe-footed workers,
stroke Shandong's thick air, the same
grayness that distant provinces inhale.

Frogs and crickets mimic the words
the infant forest whispers to the river:
We are young, you are old and tired!

Weary travelers' rumbling vehicles
clutch ever more firmly
the road's lengthening uncertainty.

Like dragons exhaling shadows,
night enfolds fatigue
and darkness befriends anticipation:

Forever the road beside the river...
Forever the river dancing away with the wind...

First Prize winner in the "Journeys" category of the 99th Ina Coolbrith Circle contest in 2018.

Alyza Lee Salomon

The Color of Bliss
(on "Pink Painting" by Kim Smith)

Breathe in this magic
stained glass window
shielding pink angels
wrestling at dawn
to build neat and perfect
cities of the future
—mapping streets and parks
and skyblue swimming pools
and luscious gardens galore—

Growing visions of
a healthy planet waking
to unfettered landscapes
via embryonic dreams—
sweet cherubs playing Candyland
while green triangular party hats
morph into redwood forests
awakening to eternal spring....

Alyza Lee Salomon

Deborah Bachels Schmidt

Deborah Bachels Schmidt lives in El Sobrante, California, with her husband, Daniel, and dog, Hazel. A member of the Marin Poetry Center and co-vice president of the Ina Coolbrith Circle, she is the author of a chapbook, *Stumbling into Grace*, published by Orchard Street Press. With Mary Eichbauer, Johanna Ely, and Laurie Hailey, she is co-author of *Love's Meditation* (Random Lane Press, 2023). She has also self-published four chapbooks. Journal credits include *Blue Unicorn, California Quarterly, The McGuffin, The Lyric,* and *The Exacting Clam*. Her poems have appeared in numerous anthologies, including *Cosmos, From Pandemic to Protest, Identity and the Self, Living Voices, Pandemic Puzzle Poems, Sunflowers,* and *Upside Down and From Below*, and have earned awards at the Poets' Dinner, the Ina Coolbrith Circle contest, and the Soul-Making Keats Literary Competition. She is a Pushcart Prize nominee and a 2022 finalist for the Malovrh-Fenlon Prize.

Dawn Chorus

He can't hear them anymore. Time was
when the bright wave of their song
washed over him each morning,
one with the golden light
as he lay in bed
still separating himself from dream,
entering the day with gladness.

Although he rarely names it,
he grieves this loss
above any other.
For himself alone,
he would accept it.
But what if it is more than
one old man's encroaching deafness?

Are the trees, the skies
being emptied of their angels?
It breaks him to think
of all that shining chorus
fading to a single, distant echo—
of all the world's children
waking to silence.

Deborah Bachels Schmidt

Sanctus

Driving home,
> *The poet lives constantly*
listening to the radio,
> *with this brave tenderness.*
she is suddenly in tears to hear
> *It is a tenderness not without fear,*
that tiny hatchling sea turtles,
> *but it can only be denied*
endangered Kemp's Ridleys,
> *at great cost.*
have been seen making their way
> *It is a vulnerability*
to the waves on the Chandeleur Islands.
> *that invites wounding, yet*
Their kind has somehow survived
> *again and again she returns,*
the great Gulf oil spill
> *he returns,*
and is nesting now
> *to life, to death, to the holy,*
on new ground,
> *sanctus, sanctus, sanctus,*
this island chain
> *arms outstretched, hearts open,*
made whole once more by human hands.
> *yes, and again yes!*

Deborah Bachels Schmidt

Stormwater

The gully on the trail has deepened
into a miniature arroyo
whose steep walls echo
with water spilling from pool to pool,
foaming at the base of each tiny fall.

My feet have forgotten
how yielding the ground can be.
Beneath new growth, saturated green,
the soft wet soil gives easily.

The landslide near the path
has washed a foot closer overnight.
Turf, heavy with rainfall,
curls downhill, upending the grasses,
exposing netted roots.

I am as drawn to the runoff
as a thirsty deer,
oblivious of the mud,
my boots soon caked with stilts of clay.

In the canyon below,
where for so long
the creekbed lay empty and silent,
silty stormwater rushes,
silvered with reflected sky.

Earth, quickening,
teaches us to receive—
open-armed, unafraid
of being washed away,
ready always to be changed.

Deborah Bachels Schmidt

Nina Serrano

Nina Serrano is an active 89-year-old poet in Vallejo, California. She produces regularly scheduled radio programs for KPFA Berkeley (94.1 FM) on literature and Latinx Affairs and for radio station KZCT (89.5 FM), known as OZCAT radio. She is retired and lives with her husband, Paul Richards. She has six grandchildren and seven great-grandchildren.

We Are In Vogue

A 106 year old Filipina is on the cover of *Vogue*
This means that we are now declared
officially "beautiful"
In the next few months and years
our shift in societal perception
will become noticeable
Less face lifts and less hair dye
Soft folds will emerge on faces rather than wrinkles
Breasts will have lowered rather than sagged
Our words will be perceived to be wise
rather than "old fashioned"
Our slipping memory will become poetic wisdom
when we can no longer be relied on
for the details of the facts
Granny styles will emerge again
Our old out-of-date dresses will become the latest retro
Retro will hold great value
as we evolve into a beauty symbol
Our involuntary naps will be declared
"beauty rest"
So we may even have to give up rest
and find the energy for our new status
as beauty queens
crowned as wise, mature, and eternally beautiful!

                                    Nina Serrano

The Maternity Ward, 1955

There were many of us
Each in her own single bed
Women recovering from childbirth
Our conversation filled the room
One mass conversation
Spontaneous and clear
in this barren white-walled ward
I was the youngest—age twenty
My first baby
The others had two or three or four
but one had twelve!
In her poverty she had no diapers waiting
But she didn't weep or complain
I was glad for my waiting packages of cloth diapers
gathered along with the other supplies
Dr. Spock had recommended
During my pregnancy I read his book over and over
No one else in the ward had read it
Reading was not a popular activity
The woman with twelve did not seem worried or upset
She hoped her church would help with her needs
I learned a lot in the conversation
Practical tips that proved so handy in the coming years
of children, grandchildren, and great-grands!

Nina Serrano

Pride in Labor

My mother worked in a luncheonette
I climbed up to a counter stool
She smiled and quickly served me a soda
Her smile of pride in her labor

At the end of the war in 1945
my father's job as a draftsman ended
He installed a drawing table, India ink, pens, and paper
in a corner of my parents' bedroom
and announced he was going to draw cartoons
which he did for the next 30 years
He smiled as he announced it
His smile of pride in his labor

My Uncle Paul used to work in a ladies garment factory
not unlike the earlier ones from the triangle fire
I would visit him there
I loved to greet the warm friendly women
at their sewing machines
I was given a magnet attached to a long string
to drag along the floor
It would attract the straight pins littering the floor
I smiled
The smile of pride in my labor.

Nina Serrano

Sherry Sheehan

Born and raised in Hawaii, Sherry Sheehan was a Las Vegas school psychologist before retiring to Crockett. She has participated in ekphrastic exhibits in Benicia, Crockett, Danville, Fairfield, Livermore, Martinez, and Rush Ranch in California, as well as in Indiana and Michigan. Michigan painter Mary Reusch and Sherry published *PoArtry*; with former Bay Area artist Robert Chapla she published *Across Currents*. Her poems are in every Benicia First Tuesday Poets anthology, all five issues of *Carquinez Poetry Review*, the eight most recent Ina Coolbrith Circle *Gatherings*, and in more than seventy issues of the *Crockett Signal*.

The Poet at Our Table

So intent was she
on what her pen was writing
and scratching out
that the poet at our table
seemed to be inside an arbor
that protected her
from all the other poetry
at the gathering.

When I peeked across the table
to glance at her evolving creation,
I saw more words her pen had blotted
than had escaped censure.
Whittled tinker-toy connectors
of thought sticks
knotted themselves in a vine-like
architecture she pruned in process,
leaving a diagram of the possibilities
her mind had pondered
that her pen had put an end to.
When she rose to read
what she had composed
in a focus that had omitted the rest of us,
her poem, excised of excess,
arrived as if it had never experienced
what I had surreptitiously witnessed.

Sherry Sheehan

Cash Slosh

Are these the last few years
that we'll use cash?

If we switch gears completely
to paying electronically,
what will happen if our e-systems crash?

At the coffee shop the other day
a nervous woman turned my way to say
she had dreamt a metaphor of just that.

Analogizing money to water,
she said she had remembered her dream
while inside her car in a car wash.

After a planetary power failure
that caused a financial tidal wave
she had felt her cash slosh.

What would happen, she asked me,
if suddenly everything everyone had saved
every country's boatload of monetary liquidity,

capsized,
and humanity's bits and bytes
were transformed into splash and spray?

I couldn't answer. I turned away
and slid my card through the e-slot
while ordering a calming latte.

Sherry Sheehan

Earth Skin

On my usual evening walk I pause for a sip of water
at a spot where I can look down the crease of a hill
into a sweating stretch of river.

Across it, on the far shore, homes and roads
ride our forgiving planet, but near me, its animal curves
remain reserved for cows and trees.

The grass covering the small muscle of hill I stand on
is gray and matted like neglected fur, and I ask
no one in particular how our planet tolerates us.

Like fleas, we give it so little peace
that I marvel it doesn't growl more often,
give a shake, and spin us off into space.

Gravity prevents that, of course,
so where we reside, burrowed in the wrinkled
topography of its bunched skin,

I guess we shouldn't be surprised
when in periodic earthquake twitches
it flexes, stretches, and scratches what itches.

                                          Sherry Sheehan

Woody Shiflett

Woody sometimes calls himself the unlikely poet. With a BS and PhD in chemical engineering and an MBA, just what is he doing writing poetry after a lifetime of technical and business writing? Simple, Woody started with poetry some 50+ years ago, gave it up for a busy career, and now returns with the loving encouragement of his much more poetically talented partner. He loves to write about life experiences and historical themes. When not dabbling in poetry, Woody finds time to consult in renewable fuels and clean energy challenges. Woody enjoys hiking, particularly along the Carquinez Strait, bicycling, kayaking and skiing; all of which inspire his writing.

Timeless

New kid in 4th grade, sparkling blue eyes, long strawberry hair
I wasn't sure why I was so intrigued except she was so fair
We played clarinet, challenged each other for 1st chair in band
By high school, warm friends still battling over top clarinet stand
Then revealed, sparkling blue eyes, long strawberry hair,
      woman in beauty blest
Why was she dating those others, I should show interest
Courage worked up, I asked her for a date
Silly boy, why did you wait so long? I can't wait.
Sharing music and poetry, ebullient young love blossomed to stay
"We've only just begun… a kiss for luck and we're on our way…"
And so we were, long walks, long talks, long kisses
Moonlight sparkling on reservoir water as it swishes
Going to the submarine races and finding passion, no subs in the dark
Reservoir police shining flashlights, asking for fishing license to park
License displayed, a wink, best wishes for fishing intents
I progressed to oboe, her, bassoon—difficult double-reed instruments
Lip muscles needed exercise, we did our best, instruments or not
The untimely loss of Dad, she my bridge over troubled waters I thought
The future shown so promising and so clear ahead
Foolish mistakes and actions not forgiven instead
We parted, decades it was, but never totally apart
Thirty-three years and reconnecting emails to start
Crazy, passionate daydreams, sparks flying and more
Dare we meet—what would be in store
A ski rendezvous, trapped in our room by unexpected rain
The passion was real, erotic, explosively insane
But, daydreams fade as we again drift away
Seventeen some years later, over a planned coffee one day
Blue eyes still sparkled, long strawberry hair now grey
So many, many memories not yet gone away

            Woody Shiflett

Beautiful woman still, with warm smile and gaze
Love and life had unfolded in their unfathomable ways
She a retired teacher, married to engineer
And me, an engineer, my partner her retired peer

'Tis the Season

Visions of a poor family called to a place of reckoning
To seek shelter where there is none but for a shed housing animals
A pending birth that would not be delayed
Signs and omens all about, shepherds surprised in the darkness
Men of wisdom, amateur astronomers,
        imagine a calling and pilgrimage
Gifts for a child born in the shed, maybe even a drum from a young boy
A tyrant's paranoia and the family now refugees
A timeless curse that strikes all too familiar a chord
When will it ever end
Believer or not, Christian, Muslim, Jew, Buddhist or what
The story catches the heart and spirit, a story of hope and prescience
Enmeshed in a world of despair and threat
Somehow enduring and more grounded in contrast
To a red-suited gnome cavorting the globe in a flying sled pulled by
        undersized reindeer
Or elves at the workbench wishing they were leprechauns
        having far more fun
No plastic angels for me, let my human ones reign all the year
And empathy for desperate families not sidelined to annual holidays
Guiding star, lead me through all the months, not just December
It's always the season....

Woody Shiflett

Rubber City Memories

Banbury mixer towers like a mechanical alien
Maw agape awaiting ration of rubber pellets and slabs
Scoop in the sulfurous vulcanizing powders
Whoosh of carbon black racing down the feed pipe
Press the cycle button and wait
Fine black talc erasing all subtleties of laborer's race
Seeping into pores to escape shower scrubs
To sweat out, greying bedsheets before next shift
Sweat, drink water, pop salt tablets, repeat.
120 degrees, night shift, lunch at 3 AM
Aspire to rise to the tradesman's ruling level: tire builder
Rotating drum, laying on sealing inner liner
Next steel belts, treads, and sidewalls
Finish with the beads and hoist onto conveyor hook
Green tire heading to curing molds
Keep the pace, keep the pace, it's piece work
Skilled mechanic technicians scurrying
      to keep machines up and running
Tool carts proudly emblazoned
      with politically incorrect badges of their Italian heritage
"De Luca—Top Wop, I go here, I go there, Dago everywhere"
Final inspection and balancing racing tires
Deep in a red brick building built before the Great War
These tires, surprisingly light, easy labor, demanding detail
Repetitive boredom broken by chatter
"I'm not the supervisor but I know how things all work here
Don't worry, I'm not coming to dinner and won't date your sister."
Channeling Sidney Poitier, black humor
      breaking ice and creating kind bonds
58,000 workers in old tire factories lining the Little Cuyahoga
Meandering down to her burning big sister and on to Lake Erie

Woody Shiflett

24 hours a day, 7 days a week
Goodyear, Firestone, Goodrich—all names America rode on
Memories now, vacant lots, shuttered factories
Morph to R&D centers, lofts and start ups
History fades except for the Oldtimers reminiscing

Woody Shiflett

Deborah Silverman

Deborah Silverman was born and raised in Washington, D.C., and has lived in many places prior to having settled in Northern California with her husband of six and a half decades. Her background includes philosophy, education, health sciences and psychology. After years of comparative silence as a psychologist, she has found, especially in these unsettled times, a measure of expression, peace, and hope in poems and in the community of poets.

Falling Back

While my head was elsewhere
        my foot found uneven space
                twisted to fit in the hollow
        I felt the turn   the fall   time suspended
Vivid anticipation of my skull smacking asphalt
Before the crash   acceptance

Sensing potential perilous descent
a lapse   a misstep   backslide   gradual decline
Unbalanced justice on uneven ground
Institutions injured   Heads elsewhere
Vivid anticipation of a failing republic
        Before the crash   acceptance

Hallelujah

For the words of Leonard Cohen
For the preacher and gospel choir
For the Book of Psalms' Hallel prayers
HALLELUJAH

For the scan clear of disease
For the baby born robust and resilient
For the aged body still with vivacious mind
HALLELUJAH

Deborah Silverman

For the stranger who pays for your groceries
For the neighbor who checks on your welfare
For the teacher who inspires your imagination
HALLELUJAH

For the woman who defies her abuser
For the leader who puts country before party
For the soldier who defends the homeland
HALLELUJAH

For the family of blood, blend, or bond
For the son or daughter who calls each day
For the love of your life still in love with you
HALLELUJAH

For the home not razed by quake or wildfire
For the child not hungry from famine
For the life not upended by war
HALLELUJAH

HALLELUJAH
For rain that quenches drought
For sunset that blazes through fog
For a world that keeps on turning

Deborah Silverman

Nature's Bite

Each spring
   drama
First bluebirds
    nesting in Melaleuca
Soon crows'
   loud calls
Preying
   eggs devoured
   fledglings taken
Crows must eat

Uneasy
   nature's claw
Rooting for underdogs
   for all babies stolen
From all
   mothers and fathers
 Accepting
    necessary inequities
Railing against
   immense
   pointless cruelties

  Deborah Silverman

Sandra D. Simmer

Sandra D. Simmer loves living her retirement years on a marina in the Bay Area near her children and new grandchildren. She enjoys activities such as writing, painting, and traveling. As a member of several northern California writing groups, Sandra explored her talent for creating poems, memoirs, and short stories. She has won local awards for her prose and poetry.

Sandra's short stories and memoirs are published in five NCPA anthologies, her poetry featured in four *Wingless Dreamer* anthologies, and her first novel *The Reclamation: Earth Under Siege* was published on Amazon in January 2023.

Fragments of Hope

Sometimes life can shatter
Our soul into jagged pieces,
Take our optimistic hearts
And turn them into shards.

Sometimes people disappoint us,
Let us down, reject our love,
Break our fragile selves
Into little bits of pain.

Sometimes we give up control,
Let others choose our life path,
Then blame them for results
When everything falls apart.

Sometimes we must take
Broken fragments of despair,
To create mosaics of hope,
And begin to live again!

Sandra D. Simmer

A Bitter Drink

Inhale air filled with voiceless chatter.
Smell the scent of those long gone.
Hear the wind's hollow laughter
While it etches memories
Into the frozen windowpane.
See flocks of geese gather
In close company
To fly to warmer climates.
When the sun moves south,
Dark clouds cool my thoughts.
I'm left to sip in silence
A bitter drink called loneliness.

Sandra D. Simmer

Used Books

The used bookshelf occupants
Are dusty, faded, worn at the edge.
Their jackets have begun to crumble,
No longer bright and shiny
Like the day they were born,
Conceived in the author's mind,
Birthed on the printer's press.

But the words upon the pages
Still shine with bold thoughts,
And delightful descriptions,
Deep thoughtful expressions,
Dialogue that warrants contemplation.
I scan the shelves for former favorites
Or new intriguing discoveries.

Old books are my good friends.
I understand their evolution.
Many aged gently over time,
Others show they were well loved.
Some barely opened, just for show.
But all still full of life to share,
If you look beneath the cover.

Sandra D. Simmer

Valerie Sopher

Valerie Sopher is grateful to *Canary*, *Caustic Frolic*, *SLANT Poetry*, *Quiet Diamonds*, *Science Write Now* and *Wingless Dreamer* (contest winner "Dawn of the Day"), among others, for publishing her work and to the Ina Coolbrith Circle for honors bestowed. Her first chapbook, *Day for Night*, is available from The Orchard Street Press. She is a singing quilter and retired lawyer who lives in the San Francisco Bay Area.

Seeking Safety

Startled geese flee
their wooded staging area
in flailing formation.
A streak of geese
across a stretched canvas sky.

Winter wind pushes me home to shelter.

Bare-branched limbs claw at the door
seeking safety from swept up air
that can kill with a breath.

Condensation forms on the window,
an empty page begging for words.
I write my story in finger scrawl,
wipe away the ending to see a line of trees
disappearing in mist.

Valerie Sopher

A Sky Divided

jet vapor trail divides   dawning sky in two
threaded seam   holds together

two halves of sky   which half are you under

one falls   one breathes
torn flag limply waves   in contagion breeze

a mask splits open   serving no purpose
you can't keep out   what shouldn't go in

sunrise   rips open the seam
half of sky   unravels

Valerie Sopher

Between Ruptures

Mid-March morning stillness
after storm furies depart.
An uneasy quiet as winter
clings to frosted rooftops.
Taut tree branches hold on tight
to what hasn't been

torn off by voracious winds.
Tulips wait to push blooms to fullness.
The garden and I brace for another round
of wind and rain without complaint,
too soon with drought maps still in yellow
even after rain rivers overflow.

Foreboding becomes a shape, bulges
beneath the surface, a sleeping
serpent under California's crust.
If I were more intuitive, I would know
what's coming, like a friend who didn't
want to take the freeway home one night.
For her, the unknown has an edge.
So we drove down streets, past faded facades,
surviving storefronts, shuttered cinemas.

I avoid freeways since the pandemic.
Nothing feels safe anymore.
I prefer stops and starts to speeding
on a highway with no horizon.
Home, I draw shutters, wait
for storms to come and pass.
Open again when the rain stops giving.

180   Valerie Sopher

Thomas Eric Stanton

Thomas Eric Stanton is primarily known as a California Surrealist. His works engage many mediums, and often emphasize the aspects of "Performance." He has produced books of poetry, and his paintings are included in many public, private, and museum collections. He lives and works in Benicia, California. He served as Poet Laureate of Benicia, California, from 2018 to 2020.

Homeland Drive

Somewhere you will find me
Playhouse in an orchard
Washing colored plastic dishes
With smaller hands
Than today's hands
All of the trees
The smell of all-season
Citrus lemon and grapefruit too
How we dreamed then
In some magic place
We would someday be
Once again
Called in for dinner
As the fireflies appeared
And each time we met
Our dreams merged
The trees boomed
Every time we played
The scent of the forest
To us so rich
So deep
So perfect
Inhaled as life itself
And never spent
That day on
Homeland drive.

Thomas Eric Stanton

Merman

She paints my wildest dreams
With the finest colored lines
And brings them to the forest
My gills blood red with the scent of bark
Hold life in Fascination
Out of water
Air gills
And her lines continue
Still to enrapture me
In this life of fantastic threading
Each day a possibility my friends
Wave so fast they form arms
And each minute she is here
My arms double to form legs
And each second she sings words
My arms grow hands
My legs grow feet
My feet learn
My gills learn
Now finally how to walk and breathe
This incredible New Life
Hands grow fingers
Fingers now holding her fingers
Our fingers.

Thomas Eric Stanton

Windflowers

How nice you sound in your name
I wonder if I've passed by you
On my walk in the morning son

Windflower
Do you have to blow
Do you have to move around
Or can you just wait
Like an empty sail
Of the boat that's taking me away

Luff
Luff windflower
Luff and swell
I don't even know what you look like
Your name is in a calendar
And the picture has been removed

I will look you up
In some dictionary still around
Somewhere
Thumb in it
Removed

Bookmark a piece of tissue
Toothpick
Incense stick burned
Half way to the nub
Odiferous genie windflower
Ah I can smell you
And I haven't even seen you

I don't even know who you are

Thomas Eric Stanton

Roger Straw

A first-generation suburban city-dweller and a privileged middle-class blue-eyed white church-going choir-boy academic, Roger dabbled in poetry from an early age without guidance or thought of publishing. Poetry was an escape, a dreamland of wanting, and a canvas for young and starry-eyed moral prescription. Through an adulthood of public service and humanitarian activism, the poetry languished some, but always surfaced, often in a hopefully more mature but persistently morally prescriptive vein. He continues to pen his life and his hopes and dreams for a more just and peaceful world.

Physics of Solace

Three dead at MSU, and five in the ICU
And more—fifty thousand students,
Six thousand faculty and staff,
And all their countless families and friends…
A vast community in loss, in shock, in recovery for years.

In the quiet of my sheltered space,
I'm a continent away from the grip and the grief,
Secure it would seem from the tv screen,
And the reality of sirens, slick spots, swarming squad cars
        and locked dorm doors,
But still, I'm in something like shock.
The story is seeded within me, the images haunt and stay.

Some fifty years ago, I passed through MSU.
I know those buildings,
Berkey Hall and the Student Union.
I walked those paths to classrooms
And sat by the Red Cedar River
And dreamed, and put together a life
Like so many there this week.

I'm called back there now
As the tv tells of terror and trauma.
I'm there. I'm there.
And it's more than rubbernecking.
For me, it's heart.

It's an inner working of overland grief…
An interpersonal PTSD…
A sharing of the physics of solace.
My family's continental spread
Is bridged in this doleful time,

                                    Roger Straw

Not only in the solid bond of bloodline and love,
But in the blood of brooding sorrow.

Benicia Depot At Sunset

My hanging lamps
Have no recourse,
But dangle in readiness
For strangers who never arrive.

I'm overhung in perfect light,
In the elegance
Of water's ebb
And land's remotion…

I see a man and dog
Gone silhouette
Like crows or waterlogs
At sun's demise.

Above, a ragged palm
Bestows farewell
On this good day.

My empty bench
Breathes and beckons,
Hums an evening song of dusky tones,
And knows so well of waiting,
Of night's descent,
And pelicans' flight
Into and beyond
The perfect light.

After Stephen Berry's painting "Depot on the Strait"

Roger Straw

She Turns to Her Own

What's under those flowing robes?
Yearning to breathe free…

What's your inner flame,
Harbored deep, yet beckoning…

Your hope shines bright for distant shores
And you dream of lives that welcome more.

Progenitor Liberty
Giving life to fleeing millions,
Your womb embraces
All who enter willingly,
Flee tyranny,
Build, for democracy,
For a land of the brave and free.

In this dark age
Of reawakening White Christian Nationalism,
Of racial and religious and political violence,
Give of yourself,
Rebirth us
With your generative loving arms
Call for us to immigrate again
To our own inherited shores.

What's under those flowing robes?
The lasting casting of promise,
The lifeblood of a borning nation,
Sometimes stilled, yet ever flowing new and free.

                                                    Roger Straw

Beth Tarpley

Beth Tarpley is a poet, retired finally from her day jobs of 40 years and living in Benicia with her husband, his two sons, and her faithful familiar, Billy, a dog who takes her everywhere with him. They roam the spaces of Benicia and many points beyond together, always returning to home and her garden.

Another Morning

Pablo's cello, unsuited at 6 a.m. sends will
rolling in creekside nettle, fragrant and stinging.
Dry phrases blow fists off the mark,
their grace to tease the welts, a dissonance
to leave a smirk flat on a face.
Tulips giving up affection
dip their dying heads low outside the vase,
admitting to their yard waste fate.
Colors blown, the fault diminuendo,
the leaves caught in a yellowing refrain.
There are the filaments, remains,
a flowery glove of space diminished.
Movement falters in low notes settled
in the dusty stars dead center in the mask,
now a memory of mornings stung with bloom.

A Witches Brew

Get out the biggest pot you own, but don't light a fire under it yet.
Summon all your tiny gods from closets and drawers,
find all your socks with holes in them.
Pick from your brain all the pictures of your favorite flowers.
Don't forget to snatch the waxing moon from the morning sky.
Cut the dress you wore to your high school prom
into tiny little pieces.
Discard the shoulder pads.
Find all of the paintings you forgot to paint,
fold them into origami cranes.

                                    Beth Tarpley

Sweep up all the dust bunnies of dog hair and forgotten dreams
from the corners of the room.
Collect all the tiny pieces of soap
you never could bear to throw away.
Search out the lost pieces of jigsaw puzzles
your children never finished.
Gather the blackened lemons from the ground around the tree
and pick all the dead paperwhites from the garden.
Pull from the shelves all the books you haven't read
but save the bird books.
Pluck all the needles from the pin cushion,
Empty the drawer in the spare room
of all the bits of fabric saved for a quilt
you don't know how to make.
On your morning walk, don't think about the dead,
pick up only twigs of manzanita
and pebbles the size of peas. Load your pockets.
Light the fire under the pot and put everything in
along with all the liquor in the all but empty bottles.
Stir frequently and add the morning's coffee grounds
for seasoning.
Cook the hell out of the unlived parts of every day
since you were born and keep stirring. This will freeze well.

Beth Tarpley

Run Away

There's always the next thing
and the next, shoehorning
into a day, shoving intent aside.
Attempts at discipline tatter,
flutter like flags above the house
pointing or marking some
loyalty or loss within the rooms below
that merely contain and require
everything all the time, the life
dedicated to their upkeep.

Shut it down, turn the furnace off
Walk out the front door.
Don't look back. Drive away
then drive some more, think about
roadways, red stop signs, the yellow signs
that warn of dangerous curves.
Keep going, not too fast to notice
the pull of the road, of gravity
the pull of tires spitting out all that
pavement in the rearview mirror.
Drive until you tire and let
your heart free the words—
those rooms that hold your life,
the wall of photos, ravens and crows
caught and framed and still
under glass, the kitchen sink full
of breakfast dishes left behind undone,
the unmade bed, the too many books
on tables and floors all read,
still holding their secrets,
the music not playing, your loved ones unfed.

Beth Tarpley

Nancy Tolin

Nancy Tolin is a California artist and writer (poetry and prose). She holds a bachelor's degree in studio art from the University of California at Davis. She exhibits her artwork in national-juried shows and contributes to newspaper poetry columns and anthologies. Often, at 3:00 am, she searches for her mischievous Muse, who delights in playing hide-and-seek games in her mind.

Lineage

We walk this Earth together
Far afield, yet so close, so wide
No matter the cultural landscape
The expansive ethnic divide

Your presence, an invisible
Companion wherever I roam
(My secret tag-along-boyfriend)
Deeply encoded in my genome

Ancient cousin, dimwit brute
Unfairly maligned far too long
Your intelligence disparaged
Archaeologists got it all wrong

Big-game hunter, maker of tools
Stocky, muscular, adaptive
Your legacy, my inheritance
Reshuffled variants deemed active

Research reveals your unforeseen traits
Artistic, compassionate, caring
Your Neanderthal DNA
I carry in my genes—timesharing

We walk this Earth together
Though you're 40,000 years extinct
My inner Neanderthal—alive
Our human connection still linked

Nancy Tolin

Sometimes a Hard Decision

Tomorrow's sun hides
And the moon falls from the sky
The shame, the shadow
Cast by SCOTUS endangers
Our freedom of choice

Today's rose-pink dawn
Cannot ignite this darkened sky
Reproductive rights
Stand noosed and hooded, prayerful
That Roe v. Wade reigns supreme

Written seven weeks before Supreme Court overturned Roe v. Wade

Haiku

Classic blue jeans caught
In unforgiving bike chain.
Ah—stylish at last.

Nancy Tolin

Diane Murray Ward

Diane is a New Yorker of West Indian heritage. She has been a modern jazz dancer/choreographer/and blog talk radio host.

She obtained an undergraduate Anthropology/Philosophy degree and interned at the United Nations, Kingsboro Psychiatric Center, and Belleview Hospital. She obtained her graduate degree in Rehabilitation Counseling. Her international work continues with NGO CSW/NY.

She has counseled abused children, disabled college students, and suicidal detainees, encouraged childhood multilingualism, homelessness abatement and supportive services for trafficked persons.

She continues several years of responsible engagement within the National Writers Union.

Her work appears in anthologies, podcasts, and open mics including: like a blot from the blue with Fin Hall, Open Minds Open Mic with Tom Colvin, Creative Expressions with Heather Archibald, BTL with Kemlyn Tan Bappe, Fixed and Free with Billy Brown, Phinnecabulary with Tricia DeJesus-Gutierrez and Art In The Basin with Amy Joy Robateau. Diane is a TESORO Artist.

Nesting Straw

I have become like a nesting straw.

Windblown, sought for as a building block, weakened at times
though still functional,

useful and rehabilitated for each avenue has climates.

I am malleable enough to provide comfort.

I have become more than nesting straw for others now realizing
the strength of fibers and strands, the strength imbued by faith and
promise by an ability to withstand

disappointment, disappearance, and choices that are not viable
otherwise, so not real choices.

I have become a building material sagging and soaked, resilient yet
fragile, steady and ready, reliable and let's not forget pliable.

I have become nesting straw fading, frayed, contorted and
exhausted. Still strong in some areas, weakened in others, useless
to some, useful to many, brave and resourceful, less blending in
belief of others, unfolding, refolding, collapsing.

Nesting straw, not necessary yet necessary with temporary
usefulness whether torn or discarded, repurposed by others, no one
knows how many times pieces are freely used, baited and finally
prohibited since it's the intentional fate of some nesting straw.

I will bind and almost blend elsewhere because I am nesting straw.
I am malleable enough to provide comfort.

                                        Diane Murray Ward

Soothing replenishes each fiber, each strand ready for the next
nest. Now each attempt wisely saving for eventual self-comfort
someplace, somewhere, sometime; for I am nesting straw and I
grow in knowledge cemented by each structure I build.

June 2023/For Singapore Poetry Festival

Diane Murray Ward

Gail Wasserman

Gail Wasserman is a poet lyricist from Benicia, California, who serves on the Benicia Literary Arts Board, and has eight publications in the "Going the Distance—Not There Yet" column of the *Benicia Herald*. Her poems have also been published by Moonstone Arts and Read or Green Books. Gail has received Honorable Mention in the Ina Coolbrith 2022 and 2023 Poetry Contests.

$5.29 Regular $5.99 Supreme

Sign says $5.29 Regular
$5.99 for Supreme Gasoline
Thought US was hell bent
On being oil independent
Fracking deep underground
Placing ugly pumps going up and down
All alongside of our once beautiful coastline

Sign says $5.29 Regular
$5.99 for Supreme Gasoline
How's a guy like me supposeda get by
And take care of my family

I'm a truck driver
Tellin' ya routes are bein' cut
Cause gas cost too much
Soon deliveries will stop
Goods won't be restocked
Today my 3 buddies were let go
Tomorrow it could be me I don't know

Sign says $5.29 Regular
$5.99 for Supreme Gasoline
How's a guy like me supposeda get by
And take care of my family

Boss says he can't make enough
After 40 years he may have to close up

Sign says $5.29 Regular
$5.99 for Supreme Gasoline
How's a guy like me supposeda get by
And take care of my family

Gail Wasserman

It's Freezing Out There

PGE you're sittin' high and mighty
Such a large company or should I say a monopoly
And us folks are layin' down on the ground
While COVID and the flu are swarmin' all around
We're left with no choice but to pay your exorbitant price
Just to stay warm on a cold winter night

PGE it's freezing out there, where's your heart?
The executives need to part
With their raises and bonuses this year
That'll lower the cost of electricity for your customers
It's freezing out there

PGE you are really hurting me
I only live in a 2 bedroom townhouse
Ouch! Ouch! Ouch!!
My December bill soared to $473
A $300 increase from the month before
And my January bill was even more
I dread to see what February will be

PGE it's freezing out there, where's your heart?
The executives need to part
With raises and bonuses this year
That'll lower the cost of electricity for your customers
It's freezing out there

PGE it's not too late, you don't have to fail as an entity
Quick send out rebate checks for electricity

PGE it's freezing out there, where's your heart?
The executives need to part
With raises and bonuses this year

Gail Wasserman

Umpqua Community College
Bang Bang Boom I'm Doomed

Bang Bang Boom I'm doomed
He just shot the professor
In the head I'm dead
Oh my God oh my God

There's nowhere to run I'm done
Oh my God oh my God oh my God
He's askin' students their faith
As if he's a member of the human race
She said she's Christian
And he shot her in the face

Bang Bang Boom
Oh my God oh my God oh my God
I don't want my life to end
Save me save my friend
We're just young students
Here to learn it's not our turn
God please please please try
We're too young to die

Bang bang boom
There's nowhere to run we're done
Oh my God oh my God oh my God
Oh my God please

Gail Wasserman

Becky Bishop White

Becky Bishop White is a third-generation Californian who spent her formative years in NYC and Cambridge, MA. At age seven, she suffered her first rejection letter from *Punch* magazine.

Fortunately, since then her poems have been in several publications and garnered awards. Of note, her poem "Flying Start" won First Prize in the 2019 Benicia Love Poetry Contest.

Becky graduated from UC Berkeley with distinction in English, but declares her writing thrived upon moving to Benicia in 2017. She especially appreciates the support from wordsmiths in Solano County and the greater Bay Area, and from the Salon sponsored by the Benicia Public Library, the First Tuesday Poets, and Benicia Literary Arts.

It's no secret that Becky considers her spouse, author James (Jim) White, her best friend, lover, and muse, and, she concludes, "Two wonderful daughters, their marvelous husbands, and a precocious grandson are the icing on the cake!"

An Afternoon of Joy

There is no gate around Robert Arneson's
verdigrised bronze sculpture of himself.
It's in a circular clearing at the end of a pathway
at the Benicia Marina.
Benicia, California, home of the late Mr. Arneson,
may he rest in eternal jollity.
Friend, feel free to sit down with him.
People run by without a glance,
but I always use the chance to pay my respects
to this artist with the irreverent humor.
In the nearby waters are those common scoters,
melanitta nigra, I learn is their scientific name,
a double-black duck, although it's a mallard atop
Arneson's driftwood headpiece.
Like a figment from a daydream,
all you see of him is his head.
The man is sticking his tongue out at you,
and he makes you smile
at his ridiculous get-up.
Arneson says, "Don't take life so seriously!
Sit down and have a laugh on me."
One of these days I will take my lunch
and sit on a nearby bench,
listen to the sheets slap the masts in clanging chorus,
accompanied by birds' squawks and honks and caws,
and the buzzing of insects among the waterweeds,
and I'll sing a paean to Robert Arneson.
Come, make merry with me.

                                        Becky Bishop White

Tempest

There was once an abandoned,
one-room schoolhouse in Maine.
It came up for auction, and my parents' bid won.
Atop a hill and above a river, it was a simple place.
No running water, no light.
No heat, save a wood stove.

Needed improvements were made
to our little vacation home,
but no modern comforts could mitigate the wind
that swelled and swirled and announced
storms from the miles-away sea.
Local children called the place "Blizzery Hill."

But no upgrade could moderate my father's anger
at life's disappointments—those accumulated slights
as the barometer of his reputation fell and fell.
He swayed in the front door, shouting under the weight
of his distress and the purchases from the state liquor store,
thundering into the gales that blustered sleet in response.

He could never win, and so he stormed, raging
all his discontents with blows both invisible and obvious.

Becky Bishop White

Song For Us

Tiki torches alight the pathway to darkness,
and warm the blood-soaked ground, long cold,
from times of bitter feuds and morals heartless,
sparked to life when slaves were sold.

The tree of death, the bigot-tree,
is what these rabid ragers again seek to grow
but those dead limbs are not our ancest-tree
and we shall overcome with the seeds we sow.

Why do some still fight this ancient battle,
when it is clear what the future will bring?
The old, tired ways will sound a death rattle
and we know the voice of Liberty will sing.

It's singing now: *"Let all flowers bloom.*
Lift up every mother, father, daughter, and son.
Stand up for your rights, shed lights on the gloom,
and we shall overcome, we shall overcome, we shall overcome!"

                                    Becky Bishop White

Previously Published Attributions

The following poems, or earlier versions, were previously published in the *Benicia Herald* column "Going The Distance:"

Claire J. Baker, "Seekers"

Ilean Baltodano, "Immigrant, Plow the Land," "The Holocaust Happened," "Black History Is the American History"

Mary Eichbauer, "Persistence"

Mary Susan Gast, "Uncertain Inalienable Rights," "Maybe Today," "Cave of Isolation"

Kathleen Herrmann, "The Day Lahaina Burned," "Unwanted"

Joanne Jagoda, "Oh, Sweet Summer" "Audacity"

Prashant Kafle, "Iron Dome"

Ramona Lappier, "I Oughta Go T'Minnesota"

Ronna Leon, "Rapping at my Door"

Nina Serrano, "Pride in Labor"

Roger Straw, "Physics of Solace," She Turns to Her Own"

Gail Wasserman, "$5.29 Regular," "It's Freezing Out There," "Umpqua Community College"

These poems, or earlier variations, were previously published as noted:

Claire J. Baker, "Border Crossing," *Blue Unicorn*, Spring 2022

Evie Groch, "Where Learning Lies," *Literary Cocktail Magazine*, Spring 2023

Kathleen Herrmann, "Unwanted," *Post-Roe Alternatives*, B Cubed Press, 2022

Sandy King, "A Gentle Arrival," *The Avocet*, Spring 2023

Alyza Lee Salomon, "The Color of Bliss," *River of Stars: Poets of the Vineyard Anthology* 2022 and on the "Laurel Leaves" page, *United Poets International*, March 2023

Becky Bishop White, "Song for Us," *Verses, Voices, & Visions of Vallejo*, 2018

Notes About the Type

Unsettled is set in Optima, a sans-serif typeface
designed by Hermann Zapf and released in
Frankfurt, West Germany in 1958. The font was
inspired by classical Roman capitals and the stone
carving on Renaissance-period tombstones Zapf
saw in Florence on a 1950 holiday to Italy.